MW00809469

Living in Hostile Territory

Ola Joseph

Living in Hostile Territory

A Survival Guide for the Overcoming Christian

By
Frederick K.C. Price, Ph.D.

Faith One Publishing
Los Angeles, California

Living in Hostile Territory
ISBN 1-883798-24-8
Copyright © 1998 by
Frederick K.C. Price, Ph.D.
P.O. Box 90000
Los Angeles, CA 90009

Published by Faith One Publishing
7901 South Vermont Avenue
Los Angeles, California 90044

Publisher's Cataloging-in-Publication
(Provided by Quality Books, Inc.)

Price, Frederick K.C.
    Living in hostile territory : a survival guide for the overcoming Christian / by Frederick K.C. Price. -- 1st ed.
    p. cm.
ISBN: 1-883798-24-8

1. Spiritual warfare. 2. Christian life--Biblical teaching. 3. Devil.   I. Title

BV4509.5.P75 1998   248.4
                                     QB198-1284

Contents

Introduction ix

1. Know the Territory 1

2. Do Not Draw Back 21

3. Conquer Your Weaknesses 31

4. Possess Your Soul 43

5. Rest in God 57

6. Manage Your Resources 75

7. Build Up Your Leaders Through Prayer 85

8. Press Toward the Mark 95

Introduction

We, as Believers, have been delivered out of the legal authority of Satan, the enemy of mankind, by being born again. However, we are still living in a world that is dominated and governed by Satan. That is why Paul tells us in 1 Timothy 6:12 to **Fight the good fight of faith.** Living in this world as a born-again, Spirit-filled, faith-walking Christian is a fight, because we are living in hostile territory.

All we have to do is look around to see what I mean. We can see people everywhere who are saved and filled with the Spirit with the evidence of speaking with other tongues, who are whipped from sunrise to sunset. They are sick and cannot pay their bills. Their marriages are on the rocks, their children are running wild, and they are frustrated.

If God were in control of the earth-realm, Christians would not be getting bombed out in life. He would not have told us through Paul to fight the good fight of faith. But God tells us to fight. This means three things. First, there is a battle we need to wage in living the faith lifestyle. Second, there is an enemy with whom we contend. Third, since Paul calls that battle **the good fight of faith,** we can win.

However, winning takes more than knowing who we are in Christ, knowing our covenant rights, and knowing how to exercise our faith to obtain the blessings available to us through our covenant. All those things are important, and we will not succeed in the things of God without them. Nevertheless, we also have to know some things about the place where we fight the good fight of faith. We need to know how to prepare ourselves for the battle.

ix

Whenever a person enters the military, the first place that person is sent after processing is to basic training, or what is commonly called "boot camp." In basic training, the recruit goes through a number of drills and exercises that prepare him or her for what to expect in a battlefield situation. The recruit is trained not only how to win, but also how to survive, because a dead soldier is no good to anyone except the enemy.

The same thing holds true when it comes to the things of God. We are no good to God or to ourselves if we do not know how to survive — we cannot fight the good fight of faith, we cannot live victoriously, and we cannot be an effective witness of the Gospel. People want to know how to win in life. If we are not winning, they will not be interested in what we have to share with them.

On top of that, the enemy is already shooting at us. He is walking around like a roaring lion, seeking whom he may devour. So if we are going to win in the things of God, we need to learn spiritual survival skills *now,* because there is literally no time like the present.

1

Know the Territory

The first thing we need to do if we want to be overcomers in Christ is to know our territory. We need to know where we live, who our enemy is, and how to keep the enemy from defeating us. Paul tells us in Colossians 1:10-13:

> that you may walk worthy of the Lord, fully pleasing Him, being fruitful in every good work and increasing in the knowledge of God;
> strengthened with all might, according to His glorious power, for all patience and longsuffering with joy;
> giving thanks to the Father who has qualified us to be partakers of the inheritance of the saints in the light.
> He has delivered us from the power of darkness and conveyed us into the kingdom of the Son of His love.

The word *power* in verse 13 actually means "dominion, rulership, domination, authority, or control." The word *dark-*

ness is being used symbolically here. Of course, the opposite of darkness is light, and the Bible uses the word *light* when it refers to God and the things related to Him.

Notice, however, that Paul says God has delivered us from the *power* of darkness. Paul does not say God has delivered us from the *presence* of darkness. That presence is still around us. Unfortunately, the presence of darkness dominates the lives of too many Christians. They live in darkness, under the dominion of satanic forces.

People in the Church have allowed the presence of darkness to so dominate their lives that they actually blame God for all the calamities that take place. This is where people outside the Church got the idea that God kills people with plagues, diseases, earthquakes, and anything else imaginable. The heavenly Father does not have a thing to do with any of those calamities. We have blamed Him for causing those tragedies because of our not knowing the structure of the world, or who is in control of it.

Do not misunderstand me here. God is in control of His family. He is directing the Body of Christ. However, the Lord is not directing the physical world around us. If He is directing this world, something is definitely wrong.

Actually, the physical world is being directed by the power of darkness. Paul tells us in 2 Corinthians 4:1-4:

> **Therefore, since we have this ministry, as we have received mercy, we do not lose heart.**
> **But we have renounced the hidden things of shame, not walking in craftiness nor handling the word of God deceitfully, but by manifestation of the truth**

2

> **commending ourselves to every man's conscience in the sight of God.**
>
> **But even if our gospel is veiled, it is veiled to those who are perishing,**
>
> **whose minds the god of this age has blinded, who do not believe, lest the light of the gospel of the glory of Christ, who is the image of God, should shine on them.**

Notice, Paul does not say "the God of all worlds," "the God of all the ages," or "God Almighty." He says, **the god of this age.** (The original King James Bible calls him "the god of this world.") The objective of this god is to blind the minds of those who have not yet believed on Jesus. That way, those people cannot come into the knowledge of Jesus Christ by accepting Him as their personal Savior and Lord. That means the god of this age must not be God or Jesus.

The god of this age is actually the individual we read about in the first chapter of Colossians — the power of darkness. He is the ruler of the darkness of this world.

In Ephesians 2:1-2, Paul adds the following:

> **And you He made alive, who were dead in trespasses and sins,**
>
> **in which you once walked according to the course of this world, according to the prince of the power of the air, the spirit who now works in the sons of disobedience.**

Notice, Paul does not say, "According to the course of God," but **... according to the course of this world**. Notice also what he calls the spirit that works in the sons of disobedience. He calls that individual **the prince of the power of the air**.

3

The word *prince* is very interesting. In the Greek, it is the word *archon,* which means "ruler" or "dominator." *The air* has to do with the atmosphere around the earth. Satan and his demon hordes are in the whole atmosphere around us, and those demonic spirits are the ones causing all the confusion in the world.

How did this enemy become so powerful? Did God create him as the prince of the power of the air, or as the god of this world? No, not really. In Genesis 1:26, we have this statement:

> **Then God said, "Let Us make man in Our image, according to Our likeness; let them have dominion over the fish of the sea, over the birds of the air, and over the cattle, over all the earth and over every creeping thing that creeps on the earth."**

The word *dominion* means "rulership, lordship, godship, controllership." God said, **"... and let them."** *Them* is plural, so it refers to all the people God would ultimately create.

God made humankind to have dominion over all the earth, but people do not have dominion over the world today. The world is actually dominating them. How did mankind lose its God-given authority?

What happened was that God made a man, Adam, and Adam became the leader of all humanity. I like to call him the federal head of the human race. God gave Adam one of the most important and priceless possessions a person can have — the freedom of choice. He gave him the right to make up his own mind.

4

However, for Adam to have something on which to exercise his choice, God gave him a prohibition. He told Adam, **"Of every tree of the garden you may freely eat; but of the tree of the knowledge of good and evil you shall not eat, for in the day that you eat of it you shall surely die"** (Genesis 2:16-17). Adam now had a choice. He could obey God, or he could obey someone else.

Adam had the power of choice, and Satan had the ability to try to influence Adam. The Lord did not create Satan to be an evil spirit, nor did He create him for the specific task of tempting Adam. Satan is really an angel. God created him as Lucifer, the son of the morning. The Bible also refers to Lucifer as the bright star (not the bright and morning star, but the bright star), and the "anointed cherub who covers."

Lucifer was the most beautiful angel the Lord had ever made. However, Lucifer became lifted up in pride. He decided he was going to be equal with God, and exalt his throne as high as the throne of God. He rebelled against the Lord, and as a result of that rebellion, Lucifer (whose name God changed to Satan) lost the estate that he originally had with God.

Satan decided he was going to get back at God. However, he realized he could not actually get back at the Lord directly, because the heavenly Father was more powerful than him. So he set up a program to try to usurp God's authority over the earth-realm.

Satan came into the garden of Eden disguised as a serpent, and appealed to man's intellect. He came to cast doubt; that is always Satan's ploy. He will always try to get you to doubt God's Word. Satan tricked Adam and Eve into transgressing God's law and, as a result, they died spiritually, turning over the dominion of this world to the devil. At that point, Satan became the god of this world.

Why didn't God take some more dust of the earth and start over by making an individual who would do what He said? Because God no longer owned the dust of the earth. Satan had actually become the legal owner of the earth. The only way God could get back into the earth-realm was by permission.

The way God got permission to re-enter the earth-realm was by having someone invite Him here. That person turned out to be Abraham. God walked up to Abraham one day, and said (and I am paraphrasing), "I am Almighty God. Follow me, and I will make you the father of many nations" (Genesis 17:1, 4). Abraham fell on the ground and said, "What do you want me to do?" From that point, God was back in business, and it was through Abraham that Jesus came.

All This Authority

Just in case you have any doubts about the devil's ownership and dominion of the world, take a look at Luke's gospel, chapter four.

Luke 4:1-7:

> **Then Jesus, being filled with the Holy Spirit, returned from the Jordan and was led by the Spirit into the wilderness,**
>
> **being tempted for forty days by the devil. And in those days He ate nothing, and afterward, when they had ended, He was hungry.**

6

And the devil said to Him, "If You are the Son of
God, command this stone to become bread."

But Jesus answered him, saying, "It is written,
'Man shall not live by bread alone, but by every word
of God.' "

Then the devil, taking Him up on a high mountain, showed Him all the kingdoms of the world in a
moment of time.

And the devil said to Him, "All this authority I
will give You, and their glory; for this has been delivered to me, and I give it to whomever I wish.

"Therefore, if You will worship before me, all
will be Yours."

Notice the words *delivered to me* in verse six. The
devil did not say, "I crept up on Adam's blind side, and
snatched the authority from him." He said someone delivered
it to him. When did the devil receive that authority? When
Adam sinned.

Someone might think at this point, "But Brother Price,
the devil was lying. The devil is a liar." It is true that the
devil is a liar, but he was not lying when he made that statement. If he were lying, then Jesus would have had to say, for
our benefit, "Devil, you're a liar. You don't have that authority, and you couldn't give it, anyhow." Jesus never argued
with the devil's ability to give Him that authority.

Luke says in verse two, **being tempted for forty days
by the devil.** A temptation is anything to which you can
yield. It is a temptation for a woman to get pregnant and
have a baby, because she is able to do so. However, it is
not a temptation for me to get pregnant, because there is no
way I can have a baby.

7

If the devil could not give Jesus the kingdoms of the world, and the power or authority over them, Satan's offer would not have been a temptation to Jesus. As I just mentioned, Jesus never argued about the devil's ability to give Him those things, so he must have had the ability to do it. That would make Satan's offer a valid temptation, and Jesus could have yielded to it, but He chose not to yield. Instead, He stayed focused on the Word of God.

Luke 4:8-13:

> **And Jesus answered and said to him, "Get behind Me, Satan! For it is written, 'You shall worship the LORD your God, and Him only you shall serve.' "**
>
> **Then he brought Him to Jerusalem, set Him on the pinnacle of the temple, and said to Him, "If You are the Son of God, throw Yourself down from here.**
>
> **For it is written:**
>
> **'He shall give His angels charge over you, To keep you,'**
>
> **"and,**
>
> **'In their hands they shall bear you up, Lest you dash your foot against a stone.' "**
>
> **And Jesus answered and said to him, "It has been said, 'You shall not tempt the LORD your God.' "**
>
> **Now when the devil had ended every temptation, he departed from Him until an opportune time.**

Jesus came out on top. He stood against the devil in every temptation, and defeated him ultimately at Calvary. Through His resurrection, He bought back and redeemed humankind, and gave us back the dominion Satan had received from Adam.

Satan has no real authority over us; we have control over the circumstances in our lives. However, the fact we are in control does not mean the devil will not shoot at us. Satan will throw anything and everything he can against us. We as Believers have the option of *not accepting* what he sends our way. We have the authority of the name of Jesus, and the covenant promises God has outlined for us in His Word. What we have to do is stand on those things, and not give the devil so much as an inch.

How Satan Has Run Over Christians

Christians have generally let Satan continue to have dominion over their lives for one of two reasons. The first explanation is that they simply did not know the devil had no legal right over them. They probably never heard about the authority of the Believer, or that they even had any rights in Christ other than salvation. Therefore, the people were ignorant of what God said was His best for their lives.

The second reason Christians have let Satan dominate them is that they have deliberately not taken advantage of their rights and authority in Christ. This is something I personally find hard to believe. Why would someone deliberately want to live in poverty, sickness, and misery, particularly when the person knows how to avoid all that mess? It would be like someone handing me 10 million dollars in cash, no strings attached, and me telling the person that I do not want the money. Think of how far 10 million dollars would go toward the proclamation of the Gospel. Think of all the lives that money would have an impact on — not to mention meeting all of a person's needs and then some.

One notion that the enemy has used to brainwash Christians into being dominated has been what the Church has taught about suffering. Traditionally, when we think of suffering, we usually think of pain, sickness, or poverty. In other words, we equate suffering with bad news in a physical sense, with being deprived in some way. There are some people who think they are supposed to suffer in the ways I have just mentioned. They think that through suffering, they will merit or actually earn the right to be in the Kingdom of God.

This idea of suffering has proved one of the biggest stumbling blocks in all Christianity. It is really a satanic doctrine. The idea was infiltrated into the Church through the pulpit by Satan to make Christians feel a sense of guilt if they did not go through some sort of deprivation. Basically, it follows the idea that surely, God is not going to just give Christians all the things He talks about in the Bible; we have to pay something for it. So the people have thought of the suffering they have gone through as a way of "balancing the scales," or evening the score between themselves and God.

All we have to do to prove how wrong this idea of suffering has been is to check out the example God has given us. We have a role model, a pattern, a blueprint as to how we should live — and that pattern is Jesus. Paul writes in Romans 8:16-17:

> **The Spirit Himself bears witness with our spirit that we are children of God,**

> **and if children, then heirs — heirs of God and**
> **joint heirs with Christ, if indeed we suffer with Him,**
> **that we may also be glorified together.**

The word *with* is the pivotal word in this verse. Paul does not say that we suffer *for* the Lord. Many Christians will say that they are "suffering for the Lord," but the reason they are suffering is that they are acting foolishly and contrary to the Word of God.

The word *with* implies that whatever Jesus has gone through, we go through. If I go to the store for my wife, that means my wife did not go to the store — I went on her behalf. If I go to the store with my wife, that means we went together. Likewise, if Paul had said that we are to suffer for the Lord, that would mean the Lord stayed home and we did the suffering. But Paul did not say *suffer for.* He said *suffer with.* In other words, Jesus is right there with us.

So how are we supposed to suffer with Jesus? To answer that question, we have to look at how Jesus suffered, and the best way to find out how Jesus suffered is to first find out how He did not suffer. Once we find out how Jesus did not suffer, that will, by process of elimination, leave us with a very clear picture of how He did suffer, and what we can expect to go through.

To the best of my knowledge, there is no passage in the Bible that says Jesus was sick, afraid, or did not have His needs met. Since Jesus did not suffer by accepting any of those things into His life, we do not have to accept any of those things into our lives either.

The fact that we do not have to suffer sickness, fear, or lack does not mean the enemy will not attack us with any of these things. It also does not mean that we are not going to open a door for the enemy to send these challenges our way. We are not perfect. We do not know everything, plus sin has compromised our faculties so they do not work as they did for Adam before he sinned. When Jesus walked the earth, He had one advantage over us. He had a mind that was untouched by sin. He had to go through the same challenges we face, and He was just as able to yield to those challenges as we are (Hebrews 4:15). However, He could perceive some things more readily than we can.

The only thing Jesus suffered when He walked the earth was persecution. That is something we cannot escape as long as we interface with humanity. We can live like hermits on top of Mount Everest, away from everyone, and the devil will never waste a shot on us, because we will not be a threat to his dominion. But if we are going to live with and around other people, we will suffer persecution.

We cannot even escape persecution if we deny Christ, because Satan is masochistic toward his children. Where do parents get the idea to mistreat their own children? A woman carries a child in her body nine months. She goes through everything a woman goes through in pregnancy and childbirth. Where does this woman get the thoughts that motivate her to abuse that child? Certainly not from God. Those thoughts come from the original child abuser — Satan.

Satan is sick. He gets a thrill out of mistreating people, and it makes no difference whether the people he mistreats are his people or God's people. The persecution that unbelievers face is different from the kind that Christians go through. They face it for a different purpose and reason, but they still have to face it. They still get their backsides kicked and their heads beaten.

The persecution Jesus faced was mainly verbal. There were several instances where the people wanted to kill Jesus before He offered Himself up as the Lamb of God for mankind. Every time the people tried to kill Him, He escaped. Jesus avoided any physical persecution that would do Him bodily harm before He could complete His mission.

Many Christians through the ages have not realized this fact, and have accepted death. During the Inquisition, in the Dark Ages, if a person expressed a belief in any church doctrine except Catholicism, the authorities put the person on the rack. They would peel the skin off that person's body as they would peel an apple. We cannot even imagine the inhumanity that one person would put upon another person "in the name of God." Many Christians placed in these circumstances thought God wanted them to die for Him, so they allowed the authorities to torture and kill them.

There is no place in the Bible that tells us to bow to the devil and let him kill us. We have records all through the New Testament where the apostles escaped death. In one instance, Paul was let down through the city wall in a large basket to escape the authorities (Acts 9:25). So we have to use enough wisdom to know when to stay in a particular situation, and when to leave. When we are dealing with people we know are going to try to kill us, we had better get away from them unless the Holy Spirit tells us otherwise. Running away from this kind of situation does not mean we are afraid. It means we are smart, because we are dealing with a ruthless enemy, Satan, who wants us dead.

Now, some situations may arise from which we cannot escape, and we may end up dying as a result. Some situations we put ourselves in may place us in harm's way, so we should go into those situations knowing the risk. In this case, we have to use our faith to believe God for preservation, and God will protect us to the point that our faith can maintain itself. But when we put ourselves into a dangerous situation, we should not think it is strange that someone is shooting at us. It is going to happen.

No matter what situation may manifest, Paul reminds us in Romans 8:18:

> **For I consider that the sufferings of this present time are not worthy to be compared with the glory which shall be revealed in us.**

It does not matter what circumstances the devil may throw at us, or the persecutions he sends our way. People can talk about us, lie about us, and make false accusations. Whatever happens is nothing compared to the glory we will receive by being faithful to the Word of God.

How We Stand — and Win

It does not matter what pretense the devil may have used for lording things over us in the past. We, as Believers, have no excuse for letting the devil continue to take advantage over us. Paul says in Ephesians 2:2-3:

> **in which you once walked according to the course of this world, according to the prince of the power of the air, the spirit who now works in the sons of disobedience,**

> **among whom also we all once conducted our-
> selves in the lusts of the flesh, fulfilling the desires of
> the flesh and of the mind, and were by nature children
> of wrath, just as the others.**

Notice the word *once*. This word indicates that the situation *once* refers back to what used to be so, but it is not so
now, or should not be so. God has made us new creatures in
Christ Jesus; therefore, we should not be living the way we
used to live. If we allow ourselves to live lives of sickness,
poverty, and defeat under the devil's authority, there is nothing God can do about it, because it is our choice.

For those of us who decide to live the way God wants
us to live, Paul admonishes in Ephesians 6:10-11:

> **Finally, my brethren, be strong in the Lord, and
> in the power of His might.**
> **Put on the whole armor of God, that you may be
> able to stand against the wiles of the devil.**

We need the armor. We cannot make it in this world by
ourselves. We need the armor on, or we are heading for a fall.
And every one of us could fall. We should never con ourselves into thinking that we are so holy, have become so su-
per-spiritual, and have gotten so many of the right tapes and
books, that we cannot fall. We are the very ones who will go
down and break our noses on the pavement if we think that.

Paul also tells us to put on *the whole armor* of God.
That means it is possible not to have all the armor on, and that
the armor of God is not one piece of equipment, but several.
If we did not need all the armor, God would not have made all

of it available to us. He also would not have told us through Paul to make sure we are wearing the complete set of armor at all times. Paul writes, **Put on the whole armor of God.** He never tells us to take off that armor; therefore, we should *keep wearing* the whole armor or God, no matter what happens in our lives.

Notice that Paul does not say God will put the armor on us. We have to do it. It is our responsibility. Since we are responsible, we cannot say, "I could not help myself," whenever we yield to temptation. According to Paul, we can help ourselves, because our wearing the whole armor of God makes us able to stand against temptation. If a person claims, "I could not help myself," and knows he or she should wear the whole armor at all times, that person is lying.

In Ephesians 6:11-12, Paul emphasizes another important point about our warfare, and reminds us of a spiritual truth no Believer should ever forget.

> **Put on the whole armor of God, that you may be able to stand against the wiles of the devil.**
>
> **For we do not wrestle against flesh and blood, but against principalities, against powers, against the rulers of the darkness of this age, against spiritual hosts of wickedness in the heavenly places.**

It is not the person across the street who is our problem, or any other individual, no matter what color their skin may be. Paul says very clearly, **For we wrestle not against flesh and blood.** Satan is our problem, but he will work through the flesh and try to manipulate us. It is our job not to let him get that far with us. It is also why Paul reminds us in Ephesians 6:13:

> **Therefore take up the whole armor of God, that you may be able to withstand in the evil day, and having done all, to stand.**

This is the second time God tells us through Paul to put on the whole armor, and the second time He tells us to stand. God wants us on our feet. He does not want us flat on our backs, or sick in bed somewhere.

Paul also reminds us that the reason we need to put on the whole armor of God is **that** [or so that] **you may be able to withstand in the evil day.** The evil day is here. Yesterday was an evil day. Today is an evil day. Tomorrow is an evil day, and the next day, and the next. The evil day is the day under which Satan dominates the world scene, and it will not cease until Jesus comes back. In the meantime, Paul instructs us in Ephesians 6:14-17:

> **Stand therefore, having girded your waist with truth, having put on the breastplate of righteousness,**
> **and having shod your feet with the preparation of the gospel of peace;**
> **above all, taking the shield of faith with which you will be able to quench all the fiery darts of the wicked one.**
> **And take the helmet of salvation, and the sword of the Spirit, which is the word of God.**

Notice, Paul says in verse 16, **above all, taking the shield of faith with which you will be able....** This is the third time Paul says we are able. He says that with the shield of faith, we will be able **to quench all the fiery darts of the wicked one.** Not just some, but all of them. This is one reason I harp so much on faith. If we do not know how to use our shield, or do not bother to use it, the darts the enemy sends are going to get through, and we will get hurt.

Why does Paul say *fiery darts?* Why didn't he just say *darts?* Because those darts will burn. Usually, when the devil sends darts our way, they will first be thoughts he plants in our minds. He will get us to ponder those thoughts, and let us smolder with passion over them. Then those things will take over, and we will become obsessed with them. With the shield of faith, we can quench those darts before they have the chance to do any damage.

This is a warfare, and we have to fight it every day, every hour, and every minute. The devil does not take holidays or weekends off, and he is out to get us any way he can. But this warfare is really the easiest thing we have ever done in our lives. The hardest thing about it with most people is their making up their minds to do it. Once an individual does that, everything is available to him — the armor, the Holy Spirit, the sword of the Spirit, which is the Word of God, and the name of Jesus. At that point, that individual has the potential for becoming a winner.

Count It All Joy

If the devil can get you to cast away our shield of faith, you will be unprotected, and he can destroy you. In the first chapter of James, we learn how we can counter the devil's efforts. James writes in verse two:

> **My brethren, count it all joy when you fall into various trials.**

James instructs us to count those things as joy. He does not say that they are joy. He just says to consider them as though they were joy. James tells us why we should do this in verse three.

> **knowing that the testing of your faith produces patience.**

Did you notice that James does not say "the testing of you"? Our faith is what is being tested, and the reason it is being tested is to see if the shield will hold under the onslaught of the fiery darts of the wicked one.

Also remember that **the testing of your faith produces patience**. In this context, *patience* means "endurance, confidence in God's ability to protect and preserve you." James goes on to say in verse four that we should **let patience have its perfect work, that** [we] **may be perfect and complete, lacking nothing.**

If we honestly think about it, the only way we will know the shield of faith will work for us is by using it. How do any of us know the car will start? By putting the key in the ignition, and starting it. We can know that your car has all the essential ingredients for it to start, but we will never personally experience the knowledge of that car starting until we start it.

The same thing goes for faith. The Bible says that the shield of faith will protect us from all the fiery darts of the wicked, but how are we going to know that? We will not know until we put up the shield of faith, and use it to stop those darts from hurting us. Only then will you have the experience or knowledge that the shield of faith works.

2

Do Not Draw Back

As vitally important as it is for us to know our territory, Paul shares something at least as important in Hebrews 10:38-39.

> "Now the just shall live by faith;
> But if anyone draws back,
> My soul has no pleasure in him."
> But we are not of those who draw back to perdi-
> tion, but of those who believe to the saving of the soul.

Notice that the word *saving* in verse 39 is in the con-
tinuous tense. Paul does not say "saved the soul," which would
indicate that our souls were already saved. *Saving* indicates
that things are in flux, that they are in process all the time.

Remember that we as human creatures are spirits, we
have souls, and we live inside physical bodies. The only part
of our threefold nature affected by the new birth is the spirit-

21

part of us, which the Bible calls the heart. The heart or spirit is the center and core of man's being. Our souls contain our minds or intellects, our emotions, our desires, and our wills — all the things that make up our personalities.

The new birth did not change our souls; neither did it change our physical bodies. This means we have to progressively work on our souls and our bodies until either we physically die or Jesus returns to the earth to set up His kingdom. When Jesus returns, two things will happen to us. First, our bodies will become like His glorified body. Second, we will receive the complete development and perfection of our souls. For all practical intents and purposes, we are saved spirit, soul and body, because Jesus has paid the price for our total redemption. However, the soul part and the physical part have not yet manifested.

The fact that we need to work on our souls as well as our bodies has proved difficult for many people to grasp. Traditionally, Christians have always talked about "saving souls." It can sound odd to say "saving spirits," even though the spirit is what we really deal with when it comes to salvation.

However, once we understand that our spirits were all changed in the new birth, it can help us to understand many of the things that are going on around us. It explains why we have certain kinds of feelings and cravings, and why we want to yield to certain kinds of temptations, even while we are thinking, "Hey, I'm a new person in Christ. I shouldn't even have that kind of thought or like that kind of thing."

Knowing only our spirits have changed can help us realize that having those feelings, cravings and temptations is normal yet governable or controllable. It is not normal in the sense of, "Hey, I'm going to do what comes naturally." No. It just means that what we may be going through is not something strange. It is par for the course.

The good news that comes with knowing only our spirits have changed is that we — that is, the real us, which are our spirits — can exercise some control over our souls and our bodies. This is why Paul tells us that **we are not of those who draw back to perdition, but of those who believe to the saving of the soul.** It is also why James says in James 1:21:

> **Therefore lay aside all filthiness and overflow of wickedness, and receive with meekness the implanted word, which is able to save your souls.**

James tells us to do something. That means filthiness does not just disappear like a snowball in the hot July sunshine. If all filthiness leaves us, it is because we have laid it aside. So if there are certain things in our lives that the Bible tags as filthy, we should look in the mirror. We are the ones who are responsible.

Notice also that James does not say to pray away all filthiness. He does not tell us to fast it away, nor to cast it out in Jesus' name. He says to lay it aside. That means we are able to do it. If we were not able, God would not require us to do it. He would not hold us accountable nor bring us into judgment for not doing it. If God tells us to do it, we can do it. The issue then becomes the will — will we do it? That is always the area of challenge.

By the Word

Notice again, in James 1:21:

Therefore lay aside all filthiness and overflow of wickedness, and receive with meekness the implanted word, which is able to save your souls.

The Word of God will change or renew our souls. However, the Word will not do us any good unless we do what it says. We are responsible for doing the Word, just as we are responsible for laying aside all filthiness.

Without the Word, we will revert to doing, saying, acting, and thinking the way we did before we met Jesus. We have really not forgotten how to do any of the ugly, negative or sinful things that we used to do. I can think of every curse word I knew and let them come out now, if I wanted. However, I choose not to use them. If we say we have forgotten how to do whatever it was that we used to do, we are really being dishonest with ourselves.

We have to stay on top of our flesh and our minds all the time. No matter how long we have been saved, walked in line with the Word, or been filled with the Spirit, situations arise that tempt us to act like our former selves. When these situations arise, we have to control our minds by staying focused on the Word of God. Controlling our minds with the Word, in turn, helps us control our bodies. The key to keeping our minds and our bodies under control is feeding our spirits with a constant diet of the Word.

It is amazing how we can understand this idea in the natural, but we do not comprehend it in the spirit. People who attend church at Chrenshaw Christian Center will say, "Well,

I've been going to Crenshaw for seven years now, and I've heard all that stuff about faith. I know all about it." So that person does not need to hear any more about faith? Fine.

Think about it this way: We have probably eaten chicken before, so we do not need to eat any more chicken for the rest of your lives. If we have eaten steak, then we do not need to eat any more steak. If we have eaten bread, we do not need to eat any more bread.

We may laugh at this idea or think it is silly, but not feeding your spirit with the Word makes as much sense as not feeding your body any physical food. The Word fuels the spirit just as food fuels the body. The food we ate a year ago will not support our bodies today. Yet, we are eating basically the same thing we did a year ago. We have to eat every day — and that is the kind of mindset we need to have with the Word. Once we set your mind in that fashion, we will look forward to "eating" the Word every day.

Paul says in Romans 12:1-2:

> **I beseech you therefore, brethren, by the mercies of God, that you present your bodies a living sacrifice, holy, acceptable to God, which is your reasonable service.**
>
> **And do not be conformed to this world, but be transformed by the renewing of your mind, that you may prove what is that good and acceptable and perfect will of God.**

Again, we need to renew our minds with the Word so that our souls can be in step with our spirits. Our spirits are actually at the head of our threefold natures. They give the plan of action to our souls. Our souls, through our bodies, should carry out the directives of our spirits.

Without our bodies, our spirits are immobile, limited in what they can do. If our souls are not in step with our spirits, we have a conflict, and that is where most people have a problem. Our souls stand in the middle, so to speak. On one side, our flesh is feeding information to our souls; and on the other side, our spirits are feeding them information. If our souls are weak, by virtue of our not renewing them with the Word, they will gravitate toward our flesh, and our actions will be fleshly oriented.

Because our souls can gravitate either toward our spirits or our flesh, the Bible makes a clear distinction between spiritually minded people and carnally minded people. *Carnal* comes from the word *carne,* which means "flesh." We can choose to let our flesh dominate us, or to let our spirits govern us. Either way, it is our decision.

Hebrews 4:12:

> **For the word of God is living and powerful, and sharper than any two-edged sword, piercing even to the division of soul and spirit, and of the joints and marrow, and is a discerner of the thoughts and intents of the heart.**

I have people come in for counseling all the time, and I tell them that I have only one answer for every problem — the Word. It worked for me, and I know that when other people work the Word, it works for them. I am not trying to play the part of a psychiatrist, and I am not trying to put down psychiatry, because it can have a place in society. What I am saying is that God has a higher and simpler method by which to help us, if we will only use it.

We do not need to go back and find out about something that happened to us as children, or relive some traumatic experience. What good is that information going to do, in and of itself? The bottom line is, what are we going to do about the situation? If we do not immerse ourselves in the Word and allow it to renew our minds, we will never have any permanent solution to our problems.

The Word will straighten us out if we let it. We are all products of our past, in that our experiences have shaped our personalities. However, we can revamp, regenerate and convert our personalities by exerting the Word of God on ourselves. The Word will help us overcome anything.

I used to have a challenge with aquaphobia — fear of water. I literally could not put my head underwater. When I got my face near some water, even in the shower, I would start suffocating and could not catch my breath.

Eventually, the Lord showed me in a flashback why I had that fear. My father had a problem with alcohol, and when he got drunk, he would try to relate to me in ways he would not do when he was sober. One day, he decided that he was going to walk out into the ocean. He put me on his shoulders and walked into the water, even though I did not want to go. The farther out we went, the more afraid I became. Finally, he dropped me into the water. Since that time, I had been afraid of going underwater.

The Lord brought that situation to my remembrance, but I overcame that fear of water by faith. There is a spirit that is behind fear, and a person can hide a fear of something behind a number of facades. To actually overcome that spirit of fear, an individual has to apply the Word of God by faith. Only the Word can effectively deal with that spirit.

Here is something else to consider: The biggest problem we have as Christians is not drinking. It is not drugs. It is not even sex. The biggest problem Christians have to deal with is in their interpersonal relationships. One Christian cannot get along with another. Why is that?

The challenge stems from the personalities of the individuals involved. Once again, the personality has nothing to do with a person's spirit. It is part of the person's soul, and can be dealt with through the Word of God — on one condition. The person must want to apply the Word to get any positive results.

A person can get a prescription from the doctor, take it home and put it in a drawer, and it will never do the person any good. It will not do him any good if he gets the prescription filled, then sets the pills on the nightstand, and just looks at them. He has to get those pills into his system, and take them as prescribed.

The same thing holds true for the Word of God. Many people have "the pill bottle" of the Word on their nightstand, or they carry it with them. They are obviously not getting that Word into their system, because their personalities are not changing. They are still as mean, ugly acting, and as overly sensitive as ever.

Hebrews 4:12-13:

> **For the word of God is living and powerful, and sharper than any two-edged sword, piercing even to**

the division of soul and spirit, and of the joints and
marrow, and is a discerner of the thoughts and intents
of the heart.

And there is no creature hidden from His [the
Word of God's] sight....

Paul is actually talking about Jesus here. Jesus is the
living Word of God. The Bible is simply a container through
which to deliver the words in it to you — words that can
change your life. Jesus said in John 6:63, "... the flesh profits nothing. The words that I speak to you are spirit, and
they are life." Those words speak life to you.

And there is no creature hidden from His sight,
but all things are naked and open to the eyes of Him to
whom we must give account.

If you are going to commit fornication, there is no point
in pulling down the shade or closing the door. Jesus is there,
and He knows what is happening. You cannot get any more
revealed than naked and open.

Your Blueprint for Living

Hebrews 4:14:

Seeing then that we have a great High Priest who
has passed through the heavens, Jesus the Son of God,
let us hold fast our confession.

What is our confession? To put it in a nutshell, our confession should be our covenant. Or, to turn the phrase around,

our covenant should be our confession. The covenant tells you who you are, what you have, and what you can do. It is your blueprint for living, and your confession it is what activates it in your life. Paul tells us to hold fast to that covenant. We would say, "Hold tight. Hold on. Don't let go."

When I first found out all this information, and started applying it to my life, I quickly learned how negatively oriented I had been. I had just said what everyone else had been saying. I found that everything that had come out of my mouth had been lodged in destruction and defeat.

Stop and look around. Everything around us in this life is negative and pessimistic. People are negative. They cannot say things without using a negative. Sometimes they use a negative like, "It scared me to death!" It is bad enough to say, "It scared me," but they have to make it even more negative to feel like they have really said something.

Start analyzing how negative people are, and make it a point to take care in what you confess. If you are not careful, you will fall back into the bad habits you practiced before; it is the easiest thing in the world to do. We may not realize what we are saying, but when we say those negative things, we add to the enemy's arsenal. Guard against giving him that advantage, and hold fast to the confession of your faith at all costs.

3

Conquer Your Weaknesses

Hebrews 4:14-15 (KJV):

> **Seeing then that we have a great high priest, that is passed into the heavens, Jesus the Son of God, let us hold fast our profession** [or literally confession].
>
> **For** [or because] **we have not an high priest which cannot be touched with the feeling of our infirmities; but was in all points tempted like as we are, yet without sin.**

Those words, to me, are some of the most encouraging words that human ears can ever hear. Because of what Paul says here, I personally cannot be discouraged any longer. Jesus can be touched with the feeling of our infirmities — *infirmities* meaning our inability to perform up to God's standard.

An infirmity can be something physical, like hearing with only one ear. Some people are infirm in the minds; they do irrational, seemingly nonsensical things to themselves and to other people. There are also all kinds of other, more subtle infirmities that people have to deal with all the time.

Paul says that we have a High Priest, Jesus, who understands what we are going through because He was tempted in all points like as we are. The reason Jesus was tempted was so He could become a merciful High Priest.

However — and some people may not be ready for this — Jesus is also a High Priest who will take no junk off us because He has already gone through it. So we cannot cop out with a bunch of lame excuses for what we may have done or want to do.

Many times, people try to exonerate themselves when they mess up. They will say things like, "Well, it would be better if I had only been able to finish college," or "If my daddy hadn't been an alcoholic, I wouldn't be like this." Jesus was tempted in all points like as we are, and He overcame every temptation. Because Jesus overcame them, we can also overcome them, no matter what the situation may be. If we want out of a particular situation, we can get out of it.

Some people do not want to get out of the situations they are in. Some people quit smoking because the doctor tells them, "If you do not stop smoking, you are going to die in six months. Your lungs are shot." They may not want to stop smoking. However, because of the fear of death the doctor has instilled in them, they quit.

There is a difference between when we stop doing something because we want to be free from it, and when we stop doing something for some other reason. There is nothing from which we cannot be free if we really want to be free. The first thing we have to do if we want to be free is confront ourselves. We have to deal with the question, "Do I really want to be free, or is it because not being free right now is so inconvenient, with everything that is going on around me?" In other words, if all those other things in our lives were not going on, would we want to be free?

Is Temptation a Sin?

One point where people have some misunderstanding is in the business of being tempted, tried or tested, and relating that to sin. A temptation, trial or test can cover a lot of territory. If you get down to the real essentials, anything that is not of faith is sin. For example, in a counseling session several years ago, a lady said to me, "I want you." In other words, she wanted me sexually. That was a temptation. If I had yielded to that temptation, I would have committed the sin of adultery.

There are other kinds of temptations, trials and tests that could still be considered sins if we yielded to them, but they are things we do not normally think of as sins. For instance, most people would not put worry in the same category as adultery, yet worry and adultery are both sins. Actually, worry is a bigger sin than adultery. When we worry, we do not believe God, and to not believe God is a definite slap in the face of our heavenly Father. In essence, we are saying that He lied.

Many people think walking by faith simply means making all the right confessions — "I believe I receive," "Whatever you desire," "Whoever will speak to the mountain." That is a part of faith, but these people do not think of all the other things that go into the faith lifestyle. Believing and not worrying are two of those things. Another is forgiving one another and not holding a grudge against anyone.

Sin is an act of our wills, and unforgiveness is sin. When someone does something that offends, upsets or hurts us, we have a choice of either holding it against that person or forgiving him. Whatever we do about the situation is up to us. Therefore, it is our responsibility to act in line with God's Word when making that choice.

Actually, when someone says or does something that hurts us, it is not that comment or action that causes us to have hurt feelings. Our emotional pain is actually *our reaction* to what happened. Whatever that person says or does may not be right, but holding it against him will not change the fact that it happened. All we will do by not forgiving him is poison ourselves.

We might as well stop praying if we harbor things against others, because God will not answer any of our prayers — even if we have everything else right in our lives. It is iniquitous to not forgive a person, ministry, or institution. The Bible says if we regard iniquity in our hearts, the Lord will not hear us (Psalm 66:18). We are not perfect, so we have no right to harbor any resentment. The only one who can find fault is God. He is the only one who has a right to do so, because He is perfect.

My position is the same as Jesus'. After they had done everything they could do to the man, He said, "Father, forgive them, for they do not know what they do" (Luke 23:34).

To learn how to forgive is perfect preventative care, spiritually speaking. I do not care what you do to me. You will never make me hold a grudge against you. I may not like what you do, and you will have only one chance to do it, but I will not go around harboring something in my heart against you.

It is also sinful to falsely accuse a brother and sister in the Lord just because of how something may appear. Instead, we should sit down, and talk with the person. Even God said in Isaiah 1:18, **"Come now, and let us reason together.... Though your sins are like scarlet, they shall be as white as snow; though they are red like crimson, they shall be as wool."**

I have found over the years that things are not always what they appear to be. A person can misread something, and go on week after week thinking what he or she misread is true. This is poison in your own cistern, and it also opens the gate for the devil to operate in other areas of your life.

Here is something else to consider. Every once in a while, I have people who want to say something because we have someone who is White in a position of authority here at the ministry. They want to start acting ugly about it.

Prejudice is an act of your will; it is not inborn. Prejudice is something you decide, and it is a sin, no matter to whom you direct the prejudice. I do not care what color a person's skin may be. If that person has a willingness, ability, and talent, and is available, I will use him — even if he has polka dots — because I do not have a problem with a person's skin color.

Some temptations we experience can seem very small, but they are still temptations. Case in point: Several years ago, I had some work done on some furniture. The company brought back the furniture after they had finished working on it. An agent from the company made sure that the work had been done to my satisfaction, then presented me with a bill.

Whenever I get a bill, I look it over to see what I am paying for. I make sure everything is right, and I am just as judicial about an undercharge as I am about an overcharge. In this case, I noticed that the company had not charged me for three of the items on which it had worked.

I pointed out this discrepancy to the agent. The agent said, "No problem." The agent knew the relationship I had with the company that had done the work, and that the company would not have minded. I told him, "I cannot pay this amount; they did not charge me enough money. I have to call them and let them know." When I called, the company told me to forget the matter. I got the work done on those three items without charge.

There was a temptation not to say anything about that undercharge. It was just a little thing, but **it is the little foxes that spoil the vines** (Song of Solomon 2:15). Each of us faces these sorts of challenges all the time.

Acting Dead to Sin

We have the capacity not to yield to temptation. As the old song reminds us, "Yield not to temptation, for yielding is sin." The Bible says Jesus was tempted. Therefore, if it is a sin to merely be tempted, Jesus sinned. *But being tempted is not a sin.* It is the yielding to temptation that is a sin. For this reason, Paul instructs us in Romans 6:11:

Likewise you also, reckon yourselves to be dead indeed to sin, but alive to God in Christ Jesus our Lord.

The word *reckon* means "to count or treat as such." We should count or treat ourselves as though we are dead, relative to sin. We are not actually dead to sin. On the contrary, we are still very much alive to it. If we were dead to sin, we would not have to count ourselves dead to it.

Let me use two illustrations to show you what I mean. One example is in the realm of personality conflicts, and the other relates to a physical situation. What I am about to share may sound raw, but sounding raw is not my intent. I am simply trying to show how we can help ourselves if the enemy tempts, tries or tests us, and to place how we can help ourselves in a context of where we live today.

Some people have problems with sex because they used to live promiscuous lives in the world. Now they want to live right, but there is something pulling on their flesh. Just think: If a man were to take a gun and shoot his penis, his penis would be dead. How many acts of sexual intercourse do you think he could then participate in? None. If a woman's vagina were dead, how many acts of fornication or adultery could that woman commit? None.

Now let's turn that illustration around to this point: If we stuck out our tongues, put that same gun up against them and pulled the trigger, our tongues would be dead. They could not gossip anymore. They could not lie. They could not run down our brothers and sisters in the Lord. They could not bear false witness. Likewise, if we put that gun against our ears and blew them away, we could not hear any more gossip. So we should act as if our tongue and our ears are dead to sin.

That is basically what God is saying through Paul in Romans 6:11. It is also what Jesus meant when He said, "If your eye offends you, pluck it out." Jesus is not saying we should physically pull our eyeballs out of their sockets. We would be destroying the temple of God if we did that. What Jesus and Paul are saying is this: When our bodies want to sin, treat them as though they are dead. Once we consider our bodies dead, and keep thinking of them that way, we will not have any more problems with sin.

Paul affirms all this in Romans 6:12 by writing:

Therefore do not let sin reign in your mortal body, that you should obey it in its lusts.

We could phrase what Paul is saying this way: Do not let sin control you. Sin cannot control you unless you let it.

Romans 6:13:

And do not present your members as instruments of unrighteousness to sin, but present yourselves as to God as being alive from the dead, and your members as instruments of righteousness to God.

Again, *your members* includes our tongues. In the sixth chapter of 1 Corinthians, Paul makes a very telling statement. He says (and I am paraphrasing), "You call yourselves Christians, and here you are, going to law against one another before the unbelievers. You are carrying out family business in the face of sinners. Why don't you just take the wrong?"

The point is, why don't we have the attitude, "Hey, my brother [or sister] meant well," and forget it? This is the kind of attitude we all ought to have.

Coming for Mercy

With all of what I have said in mind, let's go back to Hebrews 4:15, then go on to verse 16. As we did at the beginning of this chapter, I want to read this passage from the original King James Bible. There are some very important things stressed in that translation that are relevant to our discussion.

> **For we have not an high priest which cannot be touched with the feeling of our infirmities; but was in all points tempted like as we are, yet without sin.**
> **Let us therefore come boldly unto the throne of grace, that we may obtain mercy, and find grace to help in time of need.**

Whenever we mess up, we want mercy. But it is not fair for us to want mercy when we do not want to be merciful to other Christians. That is two-faced.

What about all the mess-ups we have made? Suppose God had pulled the string on us? We never think about that. If our hearts are right and we are right, nobody can hurt us. We will come out vindicated in every case. It might take some time, but we will come out on top. The Word tells us that.

The thing about Hebrews 4:16 that is so sad is that when Christians get in trouble, they tend to run *from* God instead of running *to* Him. We should run *to* the throne when we get in trouble. That is when we need mercy.

The reason we should run to the throne is that we have a High Priest who has been touched with the feeling of our infirmities. He knows what we are going through, and He is the one person we want to run to when we mess up. He is the one who can empathize with us — not sympathize, but empathize — because He has been tempted in all points like as we are, yet without sin, and He can give us mercy. Paul does not say to come crawling to the throne, to come sniveling, or to come arrogantly. He says to come boldly. That is our covenant right.

Read Hebrews 4:16 again, and notice something else that is very important.

Let us therefore come boldly unto the throne of grace, that we may obtain mercy, and find grace to help in time of need.

Mercy and grace are available for every child of God who needs them. However, we should not have to use that mercy and grace on a daily basis.

Actually, the mercy Paul is talking about in Hebrews 4:16 is like a spare tire. It is something to get us back on the road, so to speak, if we get a flat tire due to sin. We should eventually get past the point of always needing to be forgiven. We have a covenant that provides us with everything we need to live in victory.

In other words, our goal should be to live in the perfect will of God — or at least as perfect as we know how, based on the Word of God. Thank God that we can confess our sins and be forgiven. Thank God for 1 John 1:9. But we should not live in 1 John 1:9.

We ought to live in a constant state of forgiveness. We should not sulk, cry or whine over our sins three or four weeks, then go to the throne sheepishly to ask God to forgive us. A baby sulks, cries and whines. An inexperienced, immature person does that. If we sin, we should confess it instantaneously and get back in step. We should never "break our stride."

God wants us to grow. We are told in 2 Peter 3:18 to **grow in the grace and knowledge of our Lord and Savior Jesus Christ.** If we grow, we will get to the point that we will not always be at the altar confessing some sin. If we need to confess an act of sin, we should confess it. If we need to come to the altar, the altar is available — but we should get beyond having to go to the altar.

The same idea holds true for divine healing. Thank God that we can have hands laid on us. Thank God that the church can pray for us. Thank God that if we need to be anointed with oil, it is available to us. When we first find out about divine healing, being in the prayer line every week is all right. In fact, we may want to go up to have hands laid on us for agreement.

However, after we have known about divine healing for a while, we ought to be walking on our own faith feet. What happens when we are in need and the church is closed? Suppose it is a holiday — what are we going to do? We may have become so dependent on someone else to do our praying and believing for us that when the issue of praying and believing for ourselves comes up, we are helpless.

God is available to us all the time. The Holy Spirit is available to us all the time. And the Word is available to us all the time. The Word is what we need — not the church, and not the pastor. The church and the pastor have their places, but they should not take God's place.

One other thing to keep in mind is that sometimes, we are guilty of doing something wrong, but we do not want to accept the guilt. Instead, we want to exonerate ourselves, and try to push the blame on someone else.

If we are the ones at fault, we should take the responsibility like an adult for what happened. We should always be willing to admit, "Yeah, I'm capable of messing it up royally. Maybe in the eyes of the others, I missed it. Lord, help me to see it. Help me to be better. Help me to make a better shot at it next time. Open their eyes, Lord, that they may see my qualities."

I keep myself clear. I am believing God every day that my light will shine, and that people will see that light. Keep watching. I will rise to the top. I will not let anything petty get in my way. I'm totally free, and I hope you strive to be that way, too.

4

Possess Your Soul

Earlier in this book, I mentioned that we have to "save" or renew our souls by feeding them on the Word of God, and by doing what the Word says. It is something we have to do continually; it takes time and effort. That is why Jesus tells us in Luke 21:19:

"By your patience possess your souls."

Not only do we have to renew our souls, but we also have to possess them. The way we possess our souls is through patience. W.E. Vine, in his *Expository Dictionary of New Testament Words,* states it like this: "[In your patience,] ye shall gain the mastery over your souls," rather than your souls gaining mastery over you.

If we do not learn through patience to take control over our souls, it will be a tremendous enemy to our faith. Our bodies will run wild, and we will neglect our spirits.

Here is a good case in point. Americans are vastly over-weight. There is an abundance of everything to satisfy the most discriminating palate. Anything we can think that we would want, from a standpoint of tickling our taste buds, is available to us. If we go to the supermarket, the amount of food they have there is incredible.

The reason so many Americans are overweight is that their bodies run them. That, in turn, is because they have not yet possessed their souls. They have not disciplined themselves by a patient observance of, and acting on, God's Word over time. Instead of the people telling their bodies what to do, their bodies are telling them what to do.

Possessing our souls is relevant to everything in the Christian life. We cannot be circumspect and disciplined in one area physically, and dog our bodies by eating the wrong kinds of food, or by abusing our bodies in other ways. We can make all the right confessions. We can lay claim to all the scriptural texts we want. Nevertheless, if we consciously continue to abuse our flesh, we will still go down the tubes. All things being equal, we need to keep everything in its proper place. We need to learn how to take care and control of our bodies.

Now, I realize that some people are overweight because they have a glandular problem. Other people are overweight because they have a genetic predisposition. Because of these physical challenges, these people may not be able to do anything about their weight. However, most people are overweight because of what they eat. If we visited nations where masses of people starve to death, we would not see anyone starving and dropping dead at 350 pounds. Usually, the people who die of starvation are skin and bones. So generally, we are the size we are because of what we put into our bodies, and perhaps the lack of doing some other things, like exercise.

Someone could look at me, and say, "It is easy for you to talk. You're not overweight." Well, I could become overweight. I like to eat, but I control myself. For me, controlling myself is something I have to do constantly. Sometimes there will be something on my plate that is so good that I would want to do something drastic to get some more, and the devil will say, "Why don't you have some more?" So, just to show the devil that I have control, I will leave the food on the plate, and not even finish it. I do not finish my food because I cannot finish it, but just to let my body know I am in charge.

Another area where we have to control ourselves is in the area of sex. Many people become hung up with sex, especially many women — and I do not mean this as a put-down, but as an observation. There seems to be a preponderance of women who have not really come looking for God or for the Word. They came looking for a mate.

Do not misunderstand me. It is not wrong to seek a mate. God is the one who said it is not good for man to be alone (Genesis 2:18). But there is also a principle in Matthew 6:33, where Jesus says, **"But seek first the kingdom of God and His righteousness, and all these things shall be added to you."**

God knows whether or not a person wants a mate. Give Him credit for having that knowledge. But generally, a person does not want just a mate. A person wants *the right mate*. The person wants a life-partner, someone with whom to share a life, children, and everything else. If Christians do not learn to possess their souls through patience, they will be apt to get ahold of someone they will be sorry about later.

We need to use discipline. We need to learn it now, get control of ourselves, and start seeking the things of God first. The Lord will bless an unmarried Believer with a mate if that is truly what he or she is believing for. However, the person believing for that mate may not presently be in any shape to receive that person into his or her life.

Stop and think about it. What do you want for a husband or a wife? If each of us had our choice, and we picked out all the ingredients we wanted to have in a husband or wife, we would probably pick perfect ingredients. We would want someone who is right-on.

If you are not married, and God sends you Mr. or Miss Right-On, are you "right on" for that person? The man always wants the unspoiled, untouched virgin — even when he is in bed with anything that has legs on it. What about the woman he wants to make his wife? She ought to be able to say, "I have a virgin male," not just the male saying, "I have a virgin wife." It is a two-way street. So you men who have not gotten messed up yet, keep yourself pure and clean for the woman of your dreams. Be for your woman what you want the woman to be for you.

Keeping ourselves pure and clean is going to take discipline, because there are all sorts of calls coming in. The enemy makes calls all the time through our flesh, so we have to take possession of our physical bodies. I have had many opportunities to blow it. I have had women walk into my office and "put it on the desk," as it were. They were saying, "It's yours — come and get it. Yours, free." But there are no free lunches. If a person takes advantage of something like that, sooner or later, that person will pay.

Likewise, when it comes to being overweight, the key to overcoming that challenge is discipline. People who are overweight really do not need to go on a diet. What they want to do is be in control. If they have not changed their attitude about food and eating, one of two things is going to happen. They are either going to gain the pounds right back again, or they will live the rest of their lives in pure bondage, believing they cannot eat this food or that food. Besides, if diets really worked, there would not be so many of them. All a diet does is starve a person. Through that starvation, the person loses weight. If a person has not possessed his or her soul, the person is still out of control.

Control Means Victory

Here is a testimony, a good report that I would like to share with you about this area of being in control.

Dear Dr. Price:

I wanted to take this time to thank you for being so up-front with us, although sometimes, some people may feel that you come down on us too hard. But they can take it from me — it is all for our good.

Two years ago, I was weighing 270 pounds and not pleased with my life. I was working with the youth, teaching Sunday school, and embarrassed by my weight. My husband of 35 years was trying not to let on that I was an embarrassment to him, but I knew that he was ashamed of me. So when you started telling us we were hurting ourselves by allowing our appetite

47

to control us, instead of us controlling it, I thought to myself, "What does he know? Maybe we cannot help ourselves." But I soon found out differently.

I want you to know that I was wearing a size 22 and, in some things, a 24. I had to stop wearing high heels after I fell in the sanctuary one Sunday. I dropped a pen from my Bible and leaned down to pick it up, and fell. The ushers came to assist me in getting up off the floor. I can assure you this is a true story. Your lovely daughter Angela sent me a beautiful letter, expressing her concern for my well-being, and I thanked her for her concern. So I continued to come and bring my other friend (FAT) with me every Sunday. I soon stopped teaching the kids because I did not feel I could teach them self-control when I did not have any myself.

I have always admired Dr. Betty and Julie Landry for their beauty outside as well as inside. Pastor Landry and Julie have known me and my family personally for the last 10 years. I love them both very much, and it was the Landrys who encouraged me to write you. Pastor Landry said you wanted true testimonies, and I had one to share. My best friend of 34 years is a member here, and she is responsible for my being here. She, too, encouraged me to write and tell you my story.

I came through the reception line one Sunday to shake your hand and to thank you for caring about me. At that time, I had lost about 50 pounds. You told me to come back and give you another report.

I feel so good when I go shopping. I do not have to go to the "plus size" department any more. I gave all my big clothes to my sister, who refuses to do anything about her weight. I feel real good when I am out with my husband and daughter. My daughter used to call me Slim, and I felt like I was letting her down by eating myself to oblivion. She was always making me feel pretty, although I felt ugly. My top was so heavy that my bra straps had my shoulders black. I would get out of breath just walking from the parking lot to the church.

I know you hear this all the time, but I want you and Betty to know that I love you both and I am very blessed to be here. I carry my picture around with me so that people can see the difference I have made in my life. I thank you for teaching us the Holy Spirit works through doctors, because I went to a doctor to gain control of my physical life. My life is now so much better because of what I decided to do, and I have you to thank for it.

My husband and daughter are so proud of the new me. **THANK YOU FOR CARING ABOUT ME! I hope to be a part of the ministry again very soon.**

I shared this letter with the congregation one Sunday. After I read the letter, I asked if the person who wrote it was present. She was, and when she came down to the platform, the congregation gave her a round of applause.

This woman had come so far, weight-wise, from where she had started! She said that she had struggled so long with her weight, and that she had been ashamed of being so heavy. But there she was — not where she had been, and not, she said, where she was going to be when she finished losing all the extra pounds. When she made that statement, she got another round of applause from the congregation, and I told her, "Go, girl!" The woman said that when she reached her goal of being a size 10, she would be back to give another report.

The thing that especially stuck out in my mind about this woman was her height — or rather, her lack of it. To me, it was almost inconceivable that someone as short as her could carry all the extra weight that she had. But now the sister had her life together, and I loved it. Sometimes all a person needs is a little encouragement. However, you cannot help but be happy when that person experiences a major victory in his or her life.

Desiring Things

The same demonic force that assaults us in terms of sex and food will assail us in other areas as well. Take, for instance, the area of material things. Many times, when a young couple is newly married, the couple ends up letting things mess them up. Within a few years, they are in debt.

I do not care what anyone says. Debt — not having enough money, not being able to pay your bills, not being able to do some of the things you want to do for your kids — is going to affect you in every area of your life. It will touch your sex life. It will touch your frame of mind. Many times, the reason you fall into debt is that you have not learned to possess your soul. You want something and you want it now. You have not learned that there is a waiting period, a development period, to do things and buy things when you can afford to do so.

This is an area where we need a lot of discipline, because our society is geared to keep us buying. Industry is designed to make money. The only way manufacturers can make money is by customer participation, and the way they get customer participation is by making it easy for us to participate.

One way society makes buying so easy is by offering all the credit that is out in the world now. We are a credit society. The people who control the credit know that most individuals are out of control. However, the creditors make so much money on the interest from the people who pay their bills that the few who do not pay their bills or go into bankruptcy are irrelevant and immaterial. Therefore, the manufacturers and the credit-card companies do everything they can to bombard our minds, to keep us buying.

Learn to develop a relationship with your husband or wife. Get your family together. Companies will still be making cars, houses, and all kinds of electronic equipment when you can finally afford them.

In fact, to use electronics as an example, the manufacturers already have the next 10 years' worth of new modality for VCR's, televisions, and things like that. They purposely wait each season when the things come out to add another little gadget. They already have the technology now, and they could put it all on the machine. However, if they did that, everyone would buy the machine this year, and no one would want to buy it next year, or the year after that.

To keep us buying, the manufacturers operate by what is called psychological obsolescence. That means they make us psychologically dissatisfied with what we have by making a "better" one, and telling us things like, "You don't want to be left out. Everyone on the block has one. You mean you are going to go without one?" If we are not in control, we will run right out and buy one.

Another area where we have to control ourselves is in ambition. This includes status-seeking, social-climbing, and the hunger for power. We have all that among Christians, and it is sad to see.

Here is what I learned over time. We have to develop our trust in God. God knows our hearts. He knows our talents, abilities, and desires. Therefore, we should let God promote us. If He promotes us, no man can demote us. We can use this principle in anything in life, whether it is a business situation, or just a family situation.

The reason some of us may not be entrusted with any more than we have now is that we may not be ready to handle more. It is like many of the people who play the lottery. A person may win 10 million dollars, but give that person a few years, and he or she will not have a dime of that money left. You know why? Because most people do not have anything to begin with. That is why they play the lottery. They think they can get something for nothing.

Let's say a lottery ticket costs five dollars. From that five-dollar ticket, a person is supposed to win 10 million dollars. There is no justice in that rationale. Five dollars is not worth 10 million dollars.

The people running the lottery are trying to play on people's greed. Anyone who plays the lottery is not trusting the Lord. I know you may need the money. However, the reason you may need the money is that you have not possessed your soul in the area of finances.

The Cost of Impatience

The story I am about to relate is really a digression. Nevertheless, it still relates to patience and possessing your soul. I do not know the people involved, but when I first heard it, I wanted to cry. It is a true story.

Before I start, let me go back to the issue of looking for a mate. To all of the "young lovers" who are reading this book, remember this: There are no free lunches. You may think you are getting away with something but you are not. You are going to pay. Learn to chasten your own bodies, and to keep yourselves under control.

There was a young woman who went to the islands of the sea for a vacation. Of course, there are always people at vacation spots on the lookout for the frustrated, lonely American woman. This woman went to this vacation spot, and she would not wait for God to bring her a mate. She had to have someone now. She became involved with this local islander. He wined and dined her. They ended up in bed, and she knew she had found her mate.

Eventually, the woman had to go home, and she expected this man to contact her later, or get together with her. He gave her a beautifully wrapped gift, and told her not to open it until she got home. She got on the airplane, and she could not wait to open the gift. This mirrors her whole life. Each step back shows you where a person is coming from. She never should have been in that situation in the first place.

The woman opened the gift while she was on the airplane. Inside the box was a miniature casket. She opened up the casket. Inside was a little piece of paper with the words, "Welcome to the world of AIDS." She returned home, and after a little while, she was dead.

People never like for a person to talk about these things, or to be frank about them, but do you know that woman was someone's daughter? Her mother carried her inside her body nine months. That mother went through having her whole body bent out of shape with all the changes a woman goes through when she is pregnant. She gave birth to her daughter and raised her up to die from that horrible disease. Imagine the grief that mother must have gone through to have her daughter die like that.

Someone should have talked to that daughter before she went on that trip. Maybe if someone had been blunt and talked to her, she would be alive today. My advice for the unmarried is for men to keep their zippers up, and for women to keep their panties up. Is that plain enough for everyone to understand?

Do not listen to the devil's lie that there are not enough men to go around. There are plenty of men. "But they say there are five Black women to every black man." Who says a person has to marry Black? Seek the kingdom first. Develop your faith.

We read in 2 Peter 1:1-6:

> **Simon Peter, a bondservant and apostle of Jesus Christ,**
> **To those who have obtained like precious faith with us by the righteousness of our God and Savior Jesus Christ:**

Grace and peace be multiplied to you in the
knowledge of God and of Jesus our Lord,

as His divine power has given to us all things
that pertain to life and godliness, through the knowledge of Him who called us by glory and virtue,

by which have been given to us exceedingly great
and precious promises, that through these you may be
partakers of the divine nature, having escaped the cor-
ruption that is in the world through lust.

But also for this very reason, giving all dili-
gence, add to your faith virtue, to virtue knowledge,

to knowledge self-control, to self-control perseverance, to perseverance godliness.

A person could probably write a book about many kinds
of things that relate to the subject of patience, but the same
principle would apply for all of them. If we are going to walk
by faith, we have to develop the attribute of patience. We
cannot pray and get it. It is something we have to cultivate
and develop.

When we stand on God's Word over time, we will develop patience. Standing on the Word takes effort, and there
will be times when continuing to stand may seem difficult.
However, in the long run, the results will be well worth the
effort. When we develop our patience, we will, in turn, possess our souls.

5

Rest in God

Traditionally, the church has conditioned Believers to think that being a Christian is hard work, with nothing but trials, tribulations, heavy loads, and burdens. It has geared people to believe, "This life ain't worth living, this world is no good, and thank God, hallelujah, one of these days, we're going to heaven and we will be at rest."

If you are a Believer, you ought to be at rest. If God's plan were for Christians to enter into His rest when they physically died and went to heaven, then the most logical thing would be that once a person got saved, he or she would drop dead. You do not enter God's rest by dying, however. You enter His rest by living.

Jesus tells us in Matthew 11:28-30:

> **"Come to Me, all you who labor and are heavy laden, and I will give you rest.**

> "Take My yoke upon you and learn from Me, for
> I am gentle and lowly in heart, and you will find rest
> for your souls.
>
> "For My yoke is easy and My burden is light."

The reason the Christian life has traditionally been hard is that people have insisted on doing things their way instead of God's way. A Believer can do things his or her own way, and God will let that child of God labor in his own strength. But as the farmer commented, "It is a hard row to hoe."

Jesus said that if we take His yoke upon us and learn from Him, we would find rest for our souls. That is interesting. If we would think about the biggest challenges that we have had over the years, we would realize that those challenges have been soulish in nature. There are really very few spiritual problems. Most of the things we would call "spiritual problems" happen for one of two reasons. They manifest either from our not doing what God tells us to do in His Word, or from our taking some action He warns us against taking. However, when it comes to the soul area — the area of the personality, the area of the psyche of man — that is where we have all sorts of aberrations and hang-ups.

How to Enter

So how do we enter into God's rest? In the third and fourth chapters of Hebrews, Paul gives us a graphic example of what to avoid.

Hebrews 3:11:

> "So I swore in My wrath,
> 'They shall not enter My rest.'"

This verse is referring to the children of Israel. Israel missed out on the blessings of God for a 40-year period because of their unwillingness to obey the Word of God and to take the land that God had given them.

Hebrews 3:12:

> **Beware, brethren, lest there be in any of you an evil heart of unbelief in departing from the living God.**

Unbelief is evil in the sight of God.

Hebrews 3:13-14:

> **but exhort one another daily, while it is called "Today," lest any of you be hardened through the deceitfulness of sin.**
> **For we have become partakers of Christ if we hold fast to the beginning of our confidence steadfast to the end.**

Our staying in and partaking of the things of Christ are predicated on our staying in Christ and staying steadfast to the end.

Hebrews 3:15-19:

> **while it is said:**

> "Today, if you will hear His voice,
> Do not harden your hearts as in the rebellion."
>
> For who, having heard, rebelled? Indeed, was
> it not all who came out of Egypt, led by Moses?
>
> Now with whom was He angry forty years? Was
> it not with those who sinned, whose corpses fell in the
> wilderness?
>
> And to whom did He swear that they would not
> enter His rest [notice again the word *rest*], but to those
> who did not obey?
>
> So we see that they could not enter in because
> of unbelief.

The point is, nothing can keep us out of the blessings of God but unbelief. Maybe some of us did not have the advantage of going to college and obtaining a degree. Maybe some of us had to go to work at an early age. Maybe there was a separation in a person's family, and the person was left with a single parent. Maybe some of us are not what the world calls beautiful or handsome, or maybe the color of the person's skin is not right, as some would tell us in certain quarters. Thank God that none of that makes any difference when it comes to God.

Unbelief is all that kept the children of Israel out of the Promised Land. It was not the devil, nor the circumstances, nor the giants in the land — only their unbelief. We are in control of what we believe. We cannot cop out by saying we were born on the wrong side of the tracks. It does not matter even if there were no tracks in the town. We can make it if we will believe God.

Hebrews 4:1:

> **Therefore, since a promise remains of entering**
> **His rest, let us fear lest any of you seem to have come**
> **short of it.**

The Bible says that God has not given us a spirit of fear, but of power, love and a sound mind (2 Timothy 1:7). The word translated in Hebrews 4:1 as *fear* actually means "reverence, awe, respect."

Notice also that we have the same rest offered to us that God offered to Israel. He has promised it to us.

Hebrews 4:2:

> **For indeed the gospel was preached to us as well**
> **as to them....**

Wait a minute. How could the Gospel be preached to the children of Israel? Jesus had not come. He had not died. He had not risen from the dead. What does Paul mean here by *the gospel?*

The word *Gospel* literally means "good news." It is not limited to the fact that Jesus came, died and rose from the dead. These doctrinal beliefs are important to us under the New Covenant, because these beliefs are the foundation of the New Covenant. However, any time God gives us some good news, that is "gospel."

The Israelites had the Gospel — the good news — given to them. God had taken them out of slavery, and He had told them, "Hey, look across the river. The Promised Land is yours." However, notice what Paul says in the rest of Hebrews 4:2.

> **... but the word which they heard did not profit them, not being mixed with faith in those who heard it.**

The Word of God by itself will not do anything. That is why there are multitudes of people, even under great ministries, who are still living ragtag lives. They are still being defeated and whipped because they are just "sitting under the Word."

God's Word ought to profit us. We should be the better for having received it. However, the simple fact that the Word is preached is not enough to profit us. We have to make the Word profit us. In 2 Timothy 3:16, Paul writes:

> **All Scripture is given by inspiration of God, and is profitable for doctrine, for reproof, for correction, for instruction in righteousness.**

Paul does not say the Word profits us. He says it is profitable. However, we have to enter into that Word for it to profit us. How do we enter into it? In the latter part of Hebrews 4:2, Paul says:

> **... but the word which they heard did not profit them, not being mixed with faith in those who heard it.**

We enter into God's Word by mixing it with our faith. Unfortunately, in our society, everything has become fast food, fast this and fast that. People have become so accustomed to instant everything that they want instant blessings and instant success in the things of God. The things of God do not work that way.

When the Word is proclaimed, it causes faith to come — we know that from Romans 10:17. However, we have to mix the Word and our faith together, and mixing is work. We have to beat all the lumps out. We have to make everything nice and smooth. Notice, I said that *we* have to do it. We are responsible for doing the mixing. The Holy Spirit does not do it. God the Father does not do it. *We* have to do it.

How do we do this mixing? If you have ever baked anything from scratch, you probably know that you get a bowl, put the ingredients into it, and stir everything together with a spoon or an electric beater. When it comes to mixing the Word of God with our faith, the mixing bowls are our mouths, and the beater blades are our tongues. We have to speak God's Word over the issues of our lives over and over again. That is how you mix faith with the Word.

This is why I emphasize confession so much. Some people do not understand how confession works. Because they do not understand, they may think a person is bragging when that person is actually speaking the Word and keeping his or her faith built up.

We should continue to confess the Word, no matter what others may think, and not let ourselves be intimidated. We should never give in to fear or apprehension, because God has not given us a spirit of fear. He has given us a spirit of power, love, and a sound mind (2 Timothy 1:7). When we continue confessing the Word of God over our lives, we will receive the benefits God has promised us. I constantly mix the Word with my faith. Because I do that, the Lord continues to bless me.

Speaking, Hearing, Doing

We should speak the Word. When we speak the Word, we also hear it. Faith comes by hearing, and hearing by the Word of God (Romans 10:17). If we keep saying it, we will keep hearing it. If we keep hearing it, we will keep saying it. Pretty soon, that hearing and saying should influence us to do the Word.

We can tell by our actions whether or not what we say is really what we believe. There should be a place where the actions of our bodies keep step with the confessions of our mouths. Otherwise, we are only lying to ourselves. Jesus Himself tells us in Matthew 7:21, **"Not everyone who says to Me, 'Lord, Lord,' shall enter the kingdom of heaven, but he who does the will of My Father in heaven."** God's will is for us to live according to His Word.

A Scripture which further echoes this sentiment is John 14:21-24.

> **"He who has My commandments and keeps them, it is he who loves Me. And he who loves Me will be loved by My Father, and I will love him and manifest Myself to him."**
>
> **Judas (not Iscariot) said to Him, "Lord, how is it that You will manifest Yourself to us, and not to the world?"**
>
> **Jesus answered and said to him, "If anyone loves Me, he will keep My word; and My Father will love him, and We will come to him and make Our home with him.**

> "He who does not love Me does not keep My words; and the word which you hear is not Mine but the Father's who sent Me."

Notice the progression from *commandments* to *word* to *words*. All three of these terms really mean the same thing. The reason Jesus uses all three terms is so we will pick up on what He is saying.

Jesus says in John 14:21, **"He who has My commandments and keeps them, it is he who loves Me."** *Keep* means to do it. He also says in John 14:23, **"If anyone loves Me, he will keep My word."** That means if a person loves God, that person will keep God's Word. In other words, the person will do what the Word says.

It all goes back to the same principle: **Be doers of the word, and not hearers only, deceiving yourselves** (James 1:22). We are self-deceived if we hear the Word and do not do what it says.

Hebrews 4:2-4:

> For indeed the gospel was preached to us as well as to them; but the word which they heard did not profit them, not being mixed with faith in those who heard it.

> For we who have believed do enter that rest, as He has said:
> "So I swore in My wrath,
> 'They shall not enter My rest,'"
> although the works were finished from the foundation of the world.

> **For He has spoken in a certain place of the seventh day in this way: "And God rested on the seventh day from all His works."**

Notice that Paul says that we enter into God's rest. Are we resting? Are we receiving the benefit of that rest? We can enter into a restaurant, but that does not mean we will eat. We can just walk in and walk out.

It is also interesting how Paul ties together this idea of rest. The Bible says that all the works of God were finished from the foundation of the world (Hebrews 4:3). These works include the universe and salvation, since Revelation 13:8 states that Jesus Christ is the Lamb of God slain before the foundation of the world. Therefore, God has not been laboring since the foundation of the world. God has been resting, and He is asking that we enter into His rest. Whether or not we enter that rest is entirely up to us. When we rest, we are in a state of recuperating. We are not in a state of expending energy.

Hebrews 4:4-7:

> **For He has spoken in a certain place of the seventh day in this way: "And God rested on the seventh day from all His works";**
>
> **and again in this place: "They shall not enter My rest."**
>
> **Since therefore it remains that some must enter it, and those to whom it was first preached did not enter into it because of disobedience,**
>
> **again He designates a certain day, saying in David, "Today," after such a long time, as it has been said:**

"Today, if you will hear His voice,
Do not harden your hearts."

Notice especially the words *do not harden your hearts* in verse seven. That is exactly what the people of Israel did — they hardened their hearts.

How does a person harden his or her heart? In natural life, we may say, "That is a hard-hearted person." We mean the person to whom we are referring usually treats other people unkindly. However, when a person hardens his or her heart relative to the things of God, it means the person refuses to do what God says.

Christians need to be very cognizant of the following: Paul says in Hebrews 4:7, **... if you will hear His voice.** Hearing is an act of our will. Our ears are just the instruments that pick up the vibrations that travel through the air as sound. We know this fact is true because there are people present when the Word is spoken who do exactly the opposite of what the Word says.

Those people did not take the volitional act necessary to "hear" the Word by applying it to their lives. It would be a tragedy if the people said that they had heard the Word and deliberately did not do what God told them to do. What excuse could they offer to God for not having done the right thing?

By the same token, we control whether or not our hearts are hard. We cannot say life has made us hard. If life had made us hard, it would have also made everyone else hard. How can we all live in the same world and have some people get hard while others do not?

All life does is give us opportunities to harden our hearts. Our hardening our hearts is our reaction to what life offers — and the thing to which we are reacting is really not life, but the devil. God has only one thing in life, and that is abundance. Joy, peace, and all the other positive things in life are part of His order.

As I pointed out at the beginning of this book, we live in Satan's domain. He is the god of this world, and his lifestyle for everyone is misery. Satan is not happy unless people are suffering. However, he cannot indiscriminately make people suffer. He has to get people to cooperate with him.

Hebrews 4:7-9:

> **again He designates a certain day, saying in David, "Today," after such a long time, as it has been said:**
> **"Today, if you will hear His voice, Do not harden your hearts."**
> **For if Joshua had given them rest, then He would not afterward have spoken of another day.**
> **There remains therefore a rest for the people of God.**

Again, there is rest in this life. We can rest while we work — provided we learn how to mix the Gospel with faith. Two Scriptures that illustrate this idea are 1 Corinthians 3:9 and 2 Corinthians 6:1.

1 Corinthians 3:9:

> **For we are God's fellow workers; you are God's field, you are God's building.**

2 Corinthians 6:1:

> **We then, as workers together with Him also plead with you not to receive the grace of God in vain.**

The original King James Bible translates the first part of 1 Corinthians 3:9 as, **"For we are labourers together with God."** In both of these verses, the idea that Paul is trying to get across to us is that God is doing something, and He is privileging us to assist Him. God provides the power and the wherewithal. If we act in that power, we will be at rest while we are laboring.

Here is something that will clarify my point. When I was a youngster, I would see people who worked for the Department of Water & Power digging ditches. They would have to use a pick to break the hard crust of the ground so they could dig the ditch. A pick was a curved piece of metal a couple of feet long with sharp ends, attached to a handle. Swinging that pick over and over again could get to be hard work very quickly.

More recently, I have seen workers using a machine to dig a ditch. All the workers had to do was move some levers and guide the machine, and the machine would scoop out the dirt. The persons who are using the machine to dig the ditch are still working. However, what they are doing is rest compared to the people who had to swing a pick to do the same job.

When we are working in our own strength, we are using the pick. When we are working in the power of the Holy Spirit, we are using the machine.

Now, our working in the power of the Holy Spirit does not mean that we will not physically become tired. However, it is a different kind of tired than getting tired in our own ability. What we are doing will still be easy compared to our doing everything in our own strength.

Hebrews 4:10:

For he who has entered His rest has himself also ceased from his works as God did from His.

His works means your works, my works, our works. If we are in God's rest, we should have ceased from our works, just as God has ceased from His works.

Laboring to Enter?

Hebrews 4:11:

Let us therefore be diligent to enter that rest, lest anyone fall according to the same example of disobedience.

The original King James Bible translates the first part of this verse as, **"Let us labour therefore to enter into that rest."** When we talk about laboring to enter into rest, it sounds like a contradiction — until we remember that we are in spiritual warfare.

The enemy does not want us to enter into God's rest. Therefore, he will contest every inch of ground you stand on, so to speak. He wants us to be in strife. He wants us to be uptight. He wants us to be whatever else he can come up with that will cause us to be off-balance relative to the things of God.

This situation is similar to when Israel finally entered the Promised Land. Remember what we read in Hebrews about how the children of Israel refused to go into the land and provoked God. In Joshua 1:1-3, which is set 40 years after that incident, we have the following:

> **After the death of Moses the servant of the Lord, it came to pass that the Lord spoke to Joshua the son of Nun, Moses' assistant, saying:**
>
> **"Moses My servant is dead. Now therefore, arise, go over this Jordan, you and all this people, to the land which I am giving to them — the children of Israel.**
>
> **"Every place that the sole of your foot will tread upon I have given you, as I said to Moses."**

God had already given the people the land 40 years before. Once the children of Israel finally entered into it, they still had to fight. They still had to take the land. However, they took it with God's power, and with God working on their behalf.

Notice again, Joshua 1:3:

> **"Every place that the sole of your foot will tread upon I have given you, as I said to Moses."**

What God was saying was that the only thing we are going to get is the thing on which we put our feet. If we do not put our feet on it, we are not going to get it, even though He may have already given it to us.

I learned this truth many years ago. Since then, I have been putting my feet on everything I can find. I started walking, and I started confessing those things I walked on as mine. I have had opposition, but the opposition has been of no consequence.

While we are walking and confessing, Satan will set giants — demonic opposition — in front of us to frighten us, just as he initially frightened Israel. But consider this: Why were the children of Israel afraid? They were afraid because they walked by sight and not by faith. When they looked at themselves with their own eyes, they said they looked like grasshoppers (Numbers 13:33).

That is one reason Paul tells us to put on the whole armor of God (Ephesians 6:11). When we put on that armor and look in the mirror, we see God. If we keep the armor on, all the demons see is Jesus. They do not know who it is inside that armor. They think it is Jesus walking down the street. They are afraid of Jesus because the last time they met up with Him — at Calvary — He kicked their behinds.

We also need to be filled with the Holy Spirit. Without the power of the Holy Spirit, we do not stand a chance to enter into God's rest. In essence, Jesus very candidly told His disciples when He got ready to go back to heaven, "Don't you dare leave Jerusalem until you are endued with power from on High. Then you shall be witnesses unto Me" (Acts 1:4, 8). Why would Jesus tell them to wait for the power if they did not need it? And if the disciples needed that power, what makes you that think you do not need it?

There is no life any greater than the life of entering into God's rest. That is what the Christian life is all about. It is a life that we live in the fullness of God. When we live that life, we will be attractive to other people, and we will be able to influence them in coming to the Lord.

The world is looking for winners. When people see Christians who act defeated, scared, poor, frustrated, stressed-out and uptight, they do not want to hear what they may have to offer. People ought to see some victory in our lives. They ought to see some consistency, some joy, some peace, and some achievement. When they see those things, they will come to us, and we can lead them to Jesus.

6

Manage Your Resources

1 John 3:17:

> But whoever has this world's goods, and sees his
> brother in need, and shuts up his heart from him, how
> does the love of God abide in him?

The word *goods* literally means "life" or "living." It encompasses everything that has to do with livelihood — automobiles, houses, food, clothing, etc. Those things help to enhance our lives. They supply our basic needs, and give us some degree of pleasure in this world.

John goes on to say, **But whoever has this world's goods, and sees his brother in need.** The word *brother* is referring to Christians. We ought to have enough sense to know that we should do something for our earthly mothers, fathers, sisters and brothers. What Paul is talking about here goes beyond that.

As Christians, we should love one another and treat one another on an even higher level than we treat people in a blood relationship. We have the nature of our heavenly Father in us. That nature is a nature of love, and it is a nature of giving: **"For God so loved the world that He gave"** (John 3:16). God did not sit up in heaven, say, "I love you," and watch us go to hell. God's love compelled Him to act on our behalf. Since we have that same love shed abroad in our hearts, we should be willing to help when a brother or sister in Christ is in need.

This brings me to a very touchy but very important area. That is, learning to use the wisdom of God in determining how or when to help a brother or sister in the Lord who is in need. In 1 Corinthians 1:30, Paul writes:

But of Him you are in Christ Jesus, who became for us wisdom from God — and righteousness and sanctification and redemption.

Notice, Paul states, **... who became for us wisdom.** Wisdom is the ability to properly use knowledge. Even when we have knowledge about a particular situation, we may not have the wisdom to adequately use that knowledge to our advantage.

We need the wisdom of God in exercising 1 John 3:17 because people can be in need for a number of reasons. Some are in need because they want to be. Others are in need because they flagrantly disobey God's revealed Word. They absolutely refuse to do things God's way, and the end result is that they are constantly and consistently in need.

In my personal opinion and judgment, I would be a fool to give something to someone in one of those situations. My giving is only going to confirm that person in his or her waywardness. After all, why should that person shape up when he can get what he wants from me?

Here is an illustration of what I mean. There was a minister who came to see me a number of years ago. This minister had heard about what God was doing at Crenshaw Christian Center. He no doubt had observed the ministry from afar, and it looked to him as if it was prospering materially. So this minister came to me and told me all about his church.

Now, my whole purpose in life is to teach by precept and example. I am always looking for a way that I can help someone if I think I know something that can be beneficial to that person. This is not to say that I know everything. However, if someone is talking to me, and I perceive that the Lord has given me something that can help that person, I will want to share that information.

So I began to share with this brother. I said to him, "Has it occurred to you how it is that I have something that I could give you?" What I wanted to do was point him to the way the ministry had gotten to the point where he thought it could give him something. That way, he could take that information and use it himself.

This minister did not want to hear about how he could help himself. What he wanted me to do was to bring my large congregation to his little church and receive an offering for him. In other words, he wanted a freebie. I do not operate that way. God is my source, not some minister bringing his congregation to take up an offering for me. He became upset because I would not give him what he wanted. Finally, I had to ask him to leave.

Why didn't the minister ask me, "Fred, what is your secret? How can I achieve what you have achieved?" Because succeeding the way I have succeeded is work. It takes effort. It takes standing on the Word, and standing against all the criticism from people who do not understand what you are doing. That is the way God has designed the system.

I will help someone financially as the Spirit of God directs. However, I will not do so on a wholesale basis, or just because someone has a need. If you have life in your body and a head on your shoulders, you can do exactly what I did. I was willing and obedient to do what God told me to do, and He proved His Word to me. The Bible says God is no respecter of persons (Acts 10:34), so what He has done for me, He will also do for you.

We have an obligation before God to evaluate a situation, and find out why a person may be in need, before deciding whether or not to help that person. We are stewards of the things with which He has blessed us. We may have used our faith to receive what we have received, but we did not conjure up those things out of thin air. The Spirit of God brought them to us. Our blessings came as a result of our operating out of God's laws and principles. Therefore, God will hold us accountable for what we do with those blessings. We cannot simply throw away the money and goods that God has given us.

Sometimes a person needs help because he or she does not know how to operate in the Word of God or in faith. The person may not really know whom he or she is in Christ. The person may honestly want to do right, but may never have been instructed in the things of God.

I will help a person in a situation like that. I will give that person money, food, and whatever else he or she needs — along with the Word. But for someone who refuses help by telling me, "I don't want to hear about the Word — just give me some money," forget it.

God's Philosophy

In case you think what I am saying is simply my philosophy, let me outline another situation and give you Scripture. There are many people who learn about the things of God and think they do not have to work anymore. Instead of holding down a job, they live off their brothers and sisters in Christ.

The Bible does not say, "Your brother or sister in Christ shall supply all your need." It says, **And my God shall supply all your need according to His riches in glory by Christ Jesus** (Philippians 4:19). God has provided methods, such as working on a job, through which He will supply our need. Paul writes in 2 Thessalonians 3:10-15:

> **For even when we were with you, we commanded you this: If anyone will not work, neither shall he eat.**
>
> **For we hear that there are some who walk among you in a disorderly manner, not working at all, but are busybodies.**
>
> **Now those who are such we command and exhort through our Lord Jesus Christ that they work in quietness and eat their own bread.**

> **But as for you, brethren, do not grow weary in doing good.**
>
> **And if anyone does not obey our word in this epistle, note that person and do not keep company with him, that he may be ashamed.**
>
> **Yet do not count him as an enemy, but admonish him as a brother.**

Here is what Paul is saying in these verses. If a person is walking around as a busybody, getting in everyone's business, and wants to sponge off other Christians instead of holding down a job, that person should not eat. Someone may think, "That is cold. That is not acting in love." Actually, love is not conning someone, or crying over some situation. Love is when one person tells another person the truth. The information may initially shock the person at the receiving end. However, if that person will take the information to heart, it may eventually help the person deal with the situation he or she may be facing.

Understand also that what Paul says holds true for the person who is supposed to be the head of the household. If a man and wife have agreed that she will work while he goes to college and finishes getting his degree, then he is *not* the type of person Paul is talking about here. Paul is referring to the person who is supposed to be the breadwinner in the family. It does not matter whether the person is a single parent, a married person living with a spouse, or on his or her own. If that person is the one supposed to work, that person should work. Working does not mean sitting around, living off the fat of the land or sponging off Christian friends.

Notice what Paul gives as our purpose for doing what he says in 2 Thessalonians 3:10-15. He says in verse 14 that we should not keep company with that person so **that he** [the person who does not want to work] **may be ashamed.** He is not going to be ashamed if you give him what he wants.

Sometimes a person needs to be shamed. As I mentioned earlier, just giving a man or woman what he or she wants can confirm them in their error. This confirmation can eventually destroy them. Since we all have to stand on our faith feet sooner or later, our following Paul's instruction is not closing up our hearts. It is using wisdom.

We also have to use wisdom when other Christians ask us to loan them money, or when they want you to go into business with them. At Crenshaw Christian Center, we have received many, many calls through the years from people who want us to intercede for them regarding financial issues. Some of these people lent money to a church member and were not paid back. Others went into a business deal with a member and the deal went sour.

The first thing I have always wanted to say when I heard about these situations has been, "How come they didn't call the church and ask about that member before the fact?"

If the man calling had asked the church at the outset, we would probably have told him not to lend that member money, or to go into business with him. The man calling did not give the church equal time when he entered into that loan or business arrangement with that member. Therefore, it is not fair for him to expect the church to handle the situation after everything has already transpired.

If you want to give a person some money, that is one thing. When you loan a person money or go into business with them, you should know that person well. Many times, people will flake out on you. Unfortunately, that includes many people in the Body of Christ.

In Deed and in Truth

John adds in 1 John 3:18:

My little children, let us not love in word or in tongue, but in deed and in truth.

At this point, a Christian has made a decision to help someone. John is telling not only to say we will do something, but to act on what we say. In other words, we should love in action. Words will not pay bills. It will not put food on the table, nor keep the economic wolf away from the door.

Have you ever run into someone who tells you he is going to do something, and then you never see him again? Or every time you see him, he has a sheepish grin on his face, and the "help" never manifests? Personally, I do not like to deal with a person who acts that way. I can love that person from afar. I can pray for the individual, but that kind of person is really a thorn in the flesh.

We should exhibit the same integrity that God shows in dealing with us. That integrity, that God-quality of life, is inside us because Christ and the Word of God are inside us. Therefore, we should make it a point to deal with one another the way God deals with us — in honesty and in truth.

Someone once said that what a person does speaks so much louder than what that person says. Someone else said, "I can't hear what you are saying for seeing what you are doing." Once we have determined that we are going to help someone, we should follow through by doing what we say. That is how we can make sure that our lives measure up to the standard of God's Word, and let the light of that Word shine so that other people can see and follow it.

7

Build Up Your Leaders
Through Prayer

In Acts 4:18-22, the Holy Spirit shows us a situation that every Christian should take to heart. It clearly illustrates why we need to pray for our leaders, and what can happen when we do not do so. Far too many Christians have ignored or been ignorant of the fact that we need to pray and intercede for those in authority. It is a covenant right we need to exercise. It is also a spiritual survival skill we must learn to practice, particularly in light of satanic forces that would try to dominate us and stop our witness from going forth.

Before I go any further, however, let me give you a little background to the Scriptures we are going to read. Shortly after the day of Pentecost, Peter and John were going into the temple at Jerusalem to pray. There was a lame man begging at the gate called Beautiful, and they healed him in the name of Jesus. The man ran into the temple, leaping and praising God. The people inside the temple knew the man; they had undoubtedly seen him many times begging when they came to pray. Now they rejoiced with the man in what the Lord had done. However, the religious leaders soon got wind of what had happened, and they summoned Peter and John to "call them on the carpet."

> **And they** [the religious leaders] **called them** [Peter and John] **and commanded them not to speak at all nor teach in the name of Jesus.**
>
> **But Peter and John answered and said to them, "Whether it is right in the sight of God to listen to you more than to God, you judge.**
>
> **"For we cannot but speak the things which we have seen and heard."**
>
> **So when they had further threatened them, they let them go, finding no way of punishing them, because of the people, since they all glorified God for what had been done.**
>
> **For the man was over forty years old on whom this miracle of healing had been performed.**

We have a dilemma posed in this segment of Scripture. That dilemma is, "Do we obey God, or do we obey man." The religious leaders told Peter and John, "Don't teach the people any more in this name." In other words, they were telling them, "Don't preach." But Jesus had told Peter and John, along with the other apostles, **"Go into all the world and preach the gospel to every creature"** (Mark 16:15), and Jesus is the head of the Church.

Some of us may have to make a choice like the one before Peter and John. That choice may cost some of us our lives. This is why we as Believers desperately need to hold up places like this nation, the United States of America, in prayer. We need to pray for the leaders of this nation on a daily basis. We need to uplift them before God and ask Him to guide them, through the Holy Spirit, to make sound judgments and decisions. Otherwise, the devil will take full advantage of our indifference, just as he has in the past. All we have to do is look around to see that the enemy has been extremely busy.

We have a wonderful, precious opportunity in this country. We can gather together to worship the Lord and study His Word without any fear that the secret police will arrest us. People in countries with more repressive governments do not always have the freedom to proclaim the Gospel. They have been thrown into prison, and some of them have even died there.

Picture this situation: You walk out the door of the church. Someone walks up to you, and puts a submachine gun to your head. The person says, "You have two choices: No more preaching or speaking about Jesus, or go to prison for the rest of your life." I really do not ever want to be in a situation where I have to make a choice like that — do you?

Why Can't God Just Do It?

As I just mentioned, we need to pray and lift up our leaders. That way, we can make sure not to fall into situations like the one I have just illustrated. Some people may wonder, "Why can't God just act on our behalf if He cares that much about the situation? After all, He knows what is going on down here." Of course God knows, but He cannot act independent of our asking Him to intercede. It is not a case that God *does not* want to help us if we do not ask. It is a case that He *cannot*. For God to act on our benefit, we have to enable Him.

In chapter one, I mentioned that when Adam sinned, he gave legal control and ownership of this planet to Satan. That action locked God out of the earth-realm, and made Satan the god of this world. The only way God could re-enter the earth-realm to act on man's behalf was by having us invite or ask Him to do so.

Remember that when God made Adam, He formed him from the dust of the earth (Genesis 2:7). We are of this planet, so this is our home. That is why we can invite our heavenly Father into the earth-realm to work in our interest. The way we invite God is through prayer. Our inviting God allows Him, by His Spirit, to move on our behalf. It enables Him to move upon governments on behalf of His people.

Because it is our responsibility to enable God to help us, Paul gives us some very important instructions in the thirteenth chapter of Romans. We need to read these instructions very carefully. Otherwise, we will misconstrue what Paul is writing to us, and we will miss out on a very important principle. In Romans 13:1, we read:

> **Let every soul be subject to the governing authorities. For there is no authority except from God, and the authorities that exist are appointed by God.**

What exactly is Paul saying in this verse? I believe Paul is saying that God has appointed the authorities — in other words, He has appointed the offices of government on a local, state, and national level. For example, I believe that God has appointed the police force. I am not saying that God has appointed a particular person to be a police officer. What I mean is that God has appointed that there be an organization that operates as a police force. Without a police force, we cannot have an orderly society.

Our heavenly Father has appointed the offices of government. However, it is up to us to help maintain government in an orderly and godly fashion. Many times, we abdicate our responsibility as Christians. We do not become involved in areas where we can participate. One of those areas, without a doubt, is prayer. But there are also some very important activities in the natural in which we should participate.

One of those activities is voting at election time. The fact that so few Christians go to the polls is shameful, particularly in a country where we can freely vote. We should make it a point to vote in every election. We should also make sure to go before the Lord and seek Him as to whom we should vote. That way, we can make sure to elect officials who will be sensitive to the leading of God.

When we do not vote or pray for our leaders, that gives Satan the opportunity to put corrupt people in positions of government. Those corrupt people then have the opportunity to abuse the privilege of the positions they occupy. Remember that Satan is still the god of this world. He is still in charge of this world system. So even though God has appointed the offices or positions of the authorities that exist, the devil has the power and ability to influence the people placed in those positions. He also has the ability to reward them for listening to him, as well as for acting upon what he suggests.

We are all free moral agents. We can allow the devil to influence us to do evil, just as we can allow God to influence us to do good. So yes, because of satanic influence, and because we do not always pray as we should to let God influence people, there are some corrupt police officers. There are some crooked politicians, and dishonest individuals in other positions of authority. But the police force and other offices of government exist for our benefit. And I will guarantee you that, even with the few "rotten apples" we hear about, not every police officer is rotten. If every police officer were corrupt, we would all be in serious trouble.

Paul goes on in Romans 13:2-4 by writing:

> **Therefore whoever resists the authority resists the ordinance of God, and those who resist will bring judgment on themselves.**
>
> **For rulers are not a terror to good works, but to evil. Do you want to be unafraid of the authority? Do what is good, and you will have praise from the same.**
>
> **For he is God's minister to you for good. But if you do evil, be afraid; for he does not bear the sword in vain; for he is God's minister, an avenger to execute wrath on him who practices evil.**

Again, I am not saying that God necessarily appoints an individual to be a police officer. I am talking about the police force in general. Now, I believe that God can place the desire in a person's heart to select a particular career. Granted, there are people who choose a career path simply because of what they can get out of it personally or financially. These people generally do not have the welfare of society in mind when they make their choices. But I believe that, sometimes, the Lord puts it into the hearts of people to make the career choices that they make, because a person needs an anointing to fulfill a particular job.

God's Law or Man's Law?

I cannot emphasize this point enough: We need to continue to pray and believe God for a nation like this one. Here, we can practice our Christianity with impunity, and not have to put our lives on the line to worship God or to spread the Gospel. However, when there is a conflict between God's law and man's law, then we are going to have to do as Peter and John did in Acts 4:19-20:

> **But Peter and John answered and said to them, "Whether it is right in the sight of God to listen to you more than to God, you judge.**
>
> **"For we cannot but speak the things which we have seen and heard."**

Jesus had given Peter and John a command, and no command of people can abrogate the command of God. It may cost some of us something to obey God, depending on where we are on this planet. However, we as children of God have a responsibility. We cannot allow anyone to force us to not pray, not read the Bible, or not worship the Lord. We can very easily pay quite dearly to do those things if we are not careful, particularly if we do not become involved in voting and what other little things we can do. If the government takes "little" things like voting away from us, there is no telling how fast the price of prayer and worship can go up.

We can see how the devil and demons have worked through people to erode things little by little, and take God out of the fabric of society. For instance, I believe there should be prayer in the schools. It does not bother me that they do not have it there now, because the people who prayed were not praying right anyway, in terms of those prayers producing any results. However, if the government took away the right to freely pray anywhere, we would have a huge problem on our hands.

The same thing holds true for reading the Bible. We have a command from God to study to show ourselves approved unto God (2 Timothy 2:15, KJV). But if the conditions of the world are not right, we may have to pay an awful price to read our Bibles. This is why Paul writes in 1 Timothy 2:1-2:

> **Therefore I exhort first of all that supplications, prayers, intercessions, and giving of thanks be made for all men,**
>
> **for kings and all who are in authority, that we may lead a quiet and peaceable life in all godliness and reverence.**

If there are riots in the streets, or a war going on, or the military takes over the government, we will not have any peace. If we do not pray, then the leaders can do only what the devil leads them to do, because we will not have any influence over what happens. We may not be able to go to church, carry a Bible, or dare say we are Christians. So we need to pray, and hold up the leaders of our nation.

Not the Person, but the Office

When we pray for our leaders, we must not allow any personal likes or dislikes to influence us. We may not necessarily like the individuals who are our leaders. However, we are not praying for the individuals. We are praying for the positions and offices those persons occupy. When we pray, God can speak to those individuals, no matter whom they may be. He can influence them regardless of whatever doctrines they may espouse.

In the book of Daniel, Shadrach, Meshach and Abed-Nego were taken into slavery. Yet because of their steadfastness, God moved on their behalf. The Lord will cross over 27,000 people to get to one person who will dare to believe Him, and He will do wonderful things for that individual. It therefore behooves us to remain steadfast in building up our leaders through prayer.

We cannot afford to merely sit around, criticizing "those crooks in Washington," or Los Angeles, or wherever. We need to do our part so that God can move upon the offices of government. That way, the rights we enjoy as Christians and citizens can stay in effect. By our actions, we will ensure that we can live quiet and peaceable lives in all godliness and reverence.

8

Press Toward the Mark

In Philippians 3:13-14, the Apostle Paul makes a statement that should really be the marching orders for every Christian:

> **Brethren, I do not count myself to have apprehended; but one thing I do, forgetting those things which are behind and reaching forward to those things which are ahead,**
>
> **I press toward the goal for the prize of the upward call of God in Christ Jesus.**

This statement should be our constant watchword. That way, we would never become lax or self-satisfied. We would never just sit down and have the attitude that we have arrived at the grand summit of spiritual knowledge and achievement. Instead, we would continue to grow.

The kingdom of God and the things of God are so big that we could never grasp everything about it in one lifetime.

Nevertheless, we should always be reaching forth to a higher plateau. That effort pulls us above where we are already. It is a discipline we have to put ourselves through, to **press toward the goal for the prize.**

What exactly does this statement mean, however? What are the goal and the prize we are supposed to strive toward, and what does Paul mean when he says we are to press toward them? How are we supposed to achieve that goal? By what means are we supposed to achieve it? And what should be our motivation for achieving the prize?

In Philippians 3:7-12, Paul tells us exactly what our motivation should be.

> **But what things were gain to me, these I have counted loss for Christ.**
>
> **Yet indeed I also count all things loss for the excellence of the knowledge of Christ Jesus my Lord, for whom I have suffered the loss of all things, and count them as rubbish, that I may gain Christ**
>
> **and be found in Him, not having my own righteousness, which is from the law, but that which is through faith in Christ, the righteousness which is from God by faith;**
>
> **that I may know Him and the power of His resurrection, and the fellowship of His sufferings, being conformed to His death,**
>
> **if, by any means, I may attain to the resurrection from the dead.**
>
> **Not that I have already attained, or am already perfected; but I press on, that I may lay hold of that for which Christ Jesus has also laid hold of me.**

What Paul is referring to in these verses is a reciprocity, a process of "you give, I give." When Jesus obtained us, reached us, and apprehended us through the new birth, the redemptive work that He did through His death, burial, and resurrection was a success. If Jesus had done what He did and no one was ever born again, it would not have invalidated the fact that He did it. However, it would have meant that His work had not borne any fruit. When He looks at us, He can say, "I have fruit. I have evidence that what I did works."

Paul is saying, "I want to reach, apprehend, and obtain Jesus to the same extent that He has obtained, reached, and apprehended me." In other words, Paul wanted to give as much of himself for Christ as Christ had given of Himself for humanity. He wanted the evidence or fruit of that reciprocity to fully manifest in his life. That was Paul's objective, and it should also be our goal.

How could Paul meet this goal, and how can we fulfill it? By living the overcoming, victorious, godly, separated, and disciplined life of Christ. It is a life lived in accord with God's Word. It is not a shabby life like so many people live — sometimes on, sometimes off, running hot and cold — but the life of a consistent, dedicated, committed, sold-out individual. It is a Christian life lived not just in public, but all the time.

The new birth has the same import that the birth of a baby has in the natural. The idea of a woman carrying a baby nine months is not just for her to deliver the baby and leave the baby in the delivery room while she goes on with her own life. What brings glory and satisfaction to a parent is watching that baby grow up healthy and making something of himself in life. That is when a parent can say, "I have made an investment in this child, and that investment has paid off. I am proud of my handiwork."

God thinks about His children in the same way as that parent thinks about his or her child. God wants us to achieve. He wants us to put the enemy under our feet. He wants us to live the victorious life of Christ in the earth-realm to the extent that the principalities and powers will know that God lives, because God works in and through His people. Our doing those things brings glory, praise and adoration to God. He has provided the new covenant, prayer, faith, and the Holy Spirit to enable us to do that. All those things are designed for us to live that overcoming life.

Forgetting the Past

Notice again, in Philippians 3:13:

Brethren, I do not count myself to have apprehended; but one thing I do, forgetting those things which are behind and reaching forward to those things which are ahead.

Notice the words, **... forgetting those things which are behind.** If we are going to progress, go forward, achieve, we have to learn to cut ourselves loose from the past. We can draw some lessons from the past. However, we cannot look back and go forward successfully in the things of God. We have to put the past under our feet.

Satan will always try to bring up the negative things in our past to keep us from growing in the things of God. Therefore, we need to forgive ourselves of our failures and mistakes as well as to forgive other people for theirs. True forgiving includes forgetting. When a person says, "I forgive you, but I will never forget it," that person is not really practicing forgiveness. Forgiveness means letting go of whatever happened, and not picking it up again.

God is our example in forgiving and forgetting. He said in Isaiah 43:25, **"I, even I, am He who blots out your transgressions for My own sake; and I will not remember your sins."** If God does not remember it anymore, isn't that the same as saying, "I forgot it"?

We need to learn how to do that with ourselves. That is what Paul apparently learned to do, since he said, **... but one thing I do, forgetting those things which are behind.** True forgiveness is an art, and we have to work to develop it. If we do not develop it, we will remain spiritually crippled.

Forgetting those things which are behind also means forgetting the good things of the past. I can remember in my own experience when a person could buy a bottle of soda pop for five cents. However, there is no point in going to the store, standing in front of the soda pop counter, and saying, "Gee, I remember when you could buy soda pop for a nickel."

Nevertheless, some Christians insist on reminiscing in just that way when it comes to spiritual things. They want to live on some experience they had many years ago, instead of going on to achieve even greater heights. Thank God for that experience, particularly if those people learned something from it. However, we all must go on from there, or we will not grow in the things of God. We have to program our minds with something fresh and new, and set some higher goals.

People in the sports world can understand that concept. Someone may be high-jumping, and the best he has ever done is five feet 10 inches. He has never done beyond six feet, so they set the bar at six-feet-four. He misses at six-four, so they put it back down to six feet, and he makes it.

What has happened? He succeeded at jumping six feet and was not able to surpass it, but the way he did it was by shooting for a higher goal. True, he may not have achieved his objective. But if he surpassed what he did before, he could move from that point to another goal.

That is how we move and grow — step by step. However, we will not grow if we compromise ourselves by hanging on to the past.

While We Continue Pressing

Paul adds the following in Philippians 3:14:

I press toward the goal for the prize of the upward call of God in Christ Jesus.

I have already mentioned this fact earlier in this book, but I want to repeat it because it is extremely important. *Press* implies resistance — and that is what we are going to have every step of the way. The devil will have everyone on our case. He will have our spouses after us, our children complaining, and the dog, the cat and the goldfish looking strangely at us. That is not even counting the mail carrier, our supervisor and our manager at work. The devil will use anyone we know to get to us, because he knows we will listen to them a lot faster than we will listen to a complete stranger. We may suddenly wonder, "What have I done wrong? Everyone is talking about me, saying I'm crazy and putting pressure on me."

When all those things happen, remember this very important fact: It may not be what we are doing wrong that causes the opposition. The opposition may stem from what we are doing right. This is true even for salvation. In Luke 16:15-16, Jesus makes this statement:

> **And He said to them, "You are those who justify yourselves before men, but God knows your hearts. For what is highly esteemed among men is an abomination in the sight of God.**
>
> **"The law and the prophets were until John. Since that time the kingdom of God has been preached, and everyone is pressing into it."**

Notice again, the phrase *pressing into it.* Think back to the opposition that came against you to keep you from becoming a Christian. Then when you became a Christian, the opposition that came against you to keep you from being filled with the Holy Spirit. How did you obtain what you wanted? By pressing. You had to continue to go forth. You had to press in.

Satan's primary objective is to keep people out of the kingdom of God. If a person becomes born-again, Satan's secondary objective is to keep that person from being filled with the Holy Spirit. If he fails there, he has a third plan — to keep the person ignorant of who he or she is and what that person has in Christ. Satan knows that when a person learns those facts and starts living his or her life based on them, the person will grow stronger, and Satan will have a tiger by the tail. He wants to avoid that possibility at all costs.

What we have to do is learn to avoid all three of these traps Satan has laid. If we fall for any of them, he will defeat us. We must make up our minds to press or push into the things God has promised us. Jesus said in Matthew 11:12, **"And from the days of John the Baptist until now the kingdom of heaven suffers violence, and the violent take it by force."** There is someone standing in the middle of the road — Satan — who does not want us to enter the kingdom. Therefore, if we want to reap the benefits of living in the kingdom, we have to enter into it by force.

Toward the Prize

As we continue to strive, Paul says we will **press toward the goal for the prize of the upward call of God in Christ Jesus.** The way Paul phrases this statement lets us know that the prize is not conferred upon us automatically. It is something we have to obtain. Obtaining takes energy and effort, so the prize cannot be salvation, as some people have claimed. We do not press for salvation; we simply receive Jesus and acknowledge Him as our personal Savior and Lord.

The prize is also not something for the future. It is something for now, the present. Any rewards we receive for living the overcoming and victorious Christian life, such as the soul-winner's crown, will be automatically conferred upon us by Jesus Christ at the judgment seat, after the rapture. They will be the result or the reward for the life we have lived as Christians. Therefore, those rewards cannot be what Paul is talking about here.

Jesus tells us about the prize in the tenth chapter of John.

John 10:1-9:

"Most assuredly, I say to you, he who does not enter the sheepfold by the door, but climbs up some other way, the same is a thief and a robber.

"But he who enters by the door is the shepherd of the sheep.

"To him the doorkeeper opens, and the sheep hear his voice; and he calls his own sheep by name and leads them out.

"And when he brings out his own sheep, he goes before them; and the sheep follow him, for they know his voice.

"Yet they will by no means follow a stranger, but will flee from him, for they do not know the voice of strangers."

Jesus used this illustration, but they did not understand the things which He spoke to them.

Then Jesus said to them again, "Most assuredly, I say to you, I am the door of the sheep.

"All who ever came before Me are thieves and robbers, but the sheep did not hear them.

"I am the door. If anyone enters by Me, he will be saved, and...."

And implies something other than being saved. Being saved is first, it is primary, but it is not the only thing referred to here.

John 10:9-10:

"I am the door. If anyone enters by Me, he will be saved, and will go in and out and find pasture.

> **"The thief does not come except to steal, and to kill, and to destroy. I have come that they may have life, and that they may have it more abundantly."**

The life Jesus said He came to bring begins with salvation. However, there is pasture available to us within that salvation, and that pasture is an abundant life — a life circumscribed by everything we would need or desire that is consistent with a godly life. Notice how I qualify the desires here. Do not run off as some people do, and think you can have more than one spouse, or do any of the other things about which you can fantasize. Those are not things consistent with a godly life, and will not bring glory or honor to God.

The abundant life is a total lifestyle that is spiritually and materially consistent with the plan and purpose of God. It is not only obtaining material things, but obtaining material things is a part of it. Abundant life includes raising your children, being a parent, being a wife, being a husband. It includes every part of life, and it is a lifestyle that brings glory, honor and magnification to God and to the Lord Jesus Christ. I believe the **upward calling of God** Paul mentions in Philippians 3:14 is to live such a life. The only way that can be accomplished is when we win at living.

This does not mean that everything we want is going to fall into our laps all at once. Those things will manifest as quickly or as slowly as we develop our faith for receiving them. We should set some goals for ourselves, and use our faith to help reach them. We need to confess the things or solutions for which we are believing. As we share with other people, we will end up talking about it. Once we reach those objectives, we should then set some new ones. Remember that each thing we receive is not an end in itself; it is a step in reaching our ultimate goal of abundant life.

With Knowledge, Pressing Is Easy

As we strive toward manifesting God's abundance in our lives, Satan will continue to harass us and be a nuisance. However, he will not be able to stop us unless we let him. Obtaining God's abundance takes effort to win. Nevertheless, that effort is easy when we are knowledgeable in the Word, and we are operating in God's power and in His rest.

Jesus says in Matthew 11:28-30:

> **"Come to Me, all you who labor and are heavy laden, and I will give you rest.**
> **"Take My yoke upon you and learn from Me, for I am gentle and lowly in heart, and you will find rest for your souls.**
> **"For My yoke is easy and My burden is light."**

As I pointed out earlier in this book, Jesus' yoke is easy and His burden is light, compared to our trying to do everything in our own ability. People walk around with all kinds of burdens, and say, "Brother Price, will you pray for me? I am just so heavy burdened." Our carrying a heavy burden is not what Jesus is talking about in these verses. Jesus said, **"For My yoke is easy, and My burden is light."** Why does Jesus say the burden He wants us to share with Him is light? Because we are told in 1 Peter 5:7:

> **casting all your care upon Him, for He cares for you.**

If God has all our care, we do not have it. Therefore, we are free! We are carrying nothing, and nothing is light. Again, this does not mean we will not have the pressure of the enemy coming against us. Certainly, we will have to take the ground, fight for our rights, press in. However, that battle is easy when we know how to fight it, and when we know before we start fighting that we will win.

God has given us all the equipment we need to win. He has given us the privilege, the right, the power, and the knowledge. From that point, it is up to us to win.

For a complete list of books and tapes by Dr. Frederick K.C. Price, or to receive his publication, *Ever Increasing Faith Messenger,* write

Dr. Fred Price
Crenshaw Christian Center
P.O. Box 90000
Los Angeles CA 90009

BOOKS BY FREDERICK K.C. PRICE, PH.D.

HIGH FINANCE
(God Financial Plan: Tithes and Offerings)

HOW FAITH WORKS

IS HEALING FOR ALL?

HOW TO OBTAIN STRONG FAITH
Six Principles

NOW FAITH IS

THE HOLY SPIRIT —
The Missing Ingredient

FAITH, FOOLISHNESS, OR PRESUMPTION?

THANK GOD FOR EVERYTHING?

HOW TO BELIEVE GOD FOR A MATE

LIVING IN THE REALM OF THE SPIRIT

THE ORIGIN OF SATAN

CONCERNING THEM WHICH ARE ASLEEP

HOMOSEXUALITY:
State of Birth or State of Mind?

WALKING IN GOD'S WORD
Through His Promises

KEYS TO SUCCESSFUL MINISTRY

NAME IT AND CLAIM IT!
The Power of Positive Confession

THE VICTORIOUS, OVERCOMING LIFE
(A Verse-by-Verse Study on the Book of Colossians)

A NEW LAW FOR A NEW PEOPLE

THE PROMISED LAND
(A New Era for the Body of Christ)

THREE KEYS TO POSITIVE CONFESSION

THE WAY, THE WALK,
AND THE WARFARE OF THE BELIEVER
(A Verse-by-Verse Study of the Book of Ephesians)

BEWARE! THE LIES OF SATAN

TESTING THE SPIRITS

THE CHASTENING OF THE LORD

IDENTIFIED WITH CHRIST:
A Complete Cycle From Defeat to Victory

THE CHRISTIAN FAMILY:
Practical Insight for Family Living
(formerly MARRIAGE AND THE FAMILY)

THE HOLY SPIRIT:
THE HELPER WE ALL NEED

FIVE LITTLE FOXES OF FAITH

BUILDING ON A FIRM FOUNDATION

DR. PRICE'S GOLDEN NUGGETS
A Treasury of Wisdom for Both Ministers and Laypeople

About the Author

Frederick K. C. Price, Ph.D., founded Crenshaw Christian Center in Los Angeles, California, in 1973, with a congregation of some 300 people. Today, the church's membership numbers well over 18,000 members of various racial backgrounds.

Crenshaw Christian Center, home of the renowned 10,146-seat FaithDome, has a staff of more than 300 employees. Included on its 30-acre grounds are a Ministry Training Institute, the Frederick K.C. Price III elementary and junior and senior high schools, as well as the FKCP III Preschool.

The *Ever Increasing Faith* television and radio broadcasts are outreaches of Crenshaw Christian Center. The television program is viewed on more than 100 stations worldwide. The radio program airs on over 40 stations across the country and internationally.

Dr. Price travels extensively, teaching on the Word of Faith simply and understandably in the power of the Holy Spirit. He is the author of several books on faith, divine healing, prosperity, and the Holy Spirit.

In 1990, Dr. Price founded the Fellowship of Inner-City Word of Faith Ministries (FICWFM) for the purpose of fostering and spreading the faith message among independent ministries located in the metropolitan areas of the United States.